SOPHIA FAIRVIEW

Vatican´s Hidden Truths

The Secret Archives: What the Vatican Doesn't Want You to Know!

First edition

This book was professionally typeset on Reedsy.
Find out more at reedsy.com

Contents

1

Money and the Holy See: An Overview"

In the heart of Vatican City, surrounded by millennia-old cathedrals, frescoes, and statues depicting saints and angels, lies an institution that might appear incongruous to this setting—a bank. It's not just any bank, but the Vatican Bank, or as it's more formally known, the Institute for the Works of Religion (IOR). In this sanctified square mile—the world's smallest independent state—where the Pope offers blessings and cardinals debate theology, the Vatican Bank engages in activities as worldly as any Wall Street enterprise.

When one imagines the Vatican, the first images that come to mind are likely those of the Pope addressing the faithful, the majestic Sistine Chapel, or perhaps the elaborate ceremonies and rituals that have been part of Catholic tradition for centuries. Rarely does one picture a group of suited individuals poring over balance sheets or discussing investment portfolios. Yet, it's precisely this juxtaposition—the sacred and the profane, the spiritual and the material—that makes the Vatican Bank a fascinating subject of study.

Historical Backdrop

The Vatican Bank was established during World War II, in 1942, by Pope Pius XII. While its ostensible mission is to provide for the religious or charitable works and initiatives endorsed by the Holy See, its operations have often ventured into complex and sometimes murky waters. Over the years, the bank has been involved in a host of financial transactions, both ordinary and extraordinary, that have caught the attention of financial regulators, historians, and even conspiracy theorists.

A Unique Institution

What sets the Vatican Bank apart from other banking institutions? For starters, it's one of the few banks in the world that allows transactions in Latin. Jokes aside, its unique status as a non-commercial bank that operates within a sovereign territory but isn't regulated by it creates a peculiar operating environment. Its clients are typically state officials, clergy, and certain Catholic institutions, but the range of its financial operations often surpasses these boundaries.

Financial Sanctity or Complexity?

To the outside world, the Vatican Bank seems shrouded in mystery. Partially, this is because the bank is not required to disclose as much information as commercial banks, given its non-commercial status and jurisdictional peculiarities. While it has taken steps to improve transparency in recent years, questions still linger about its past dealings, including accusations of money laundering, corruption, and involvement in the financing of covert operations.

Conclusion

Understanding the Vatican Bank is essential for grasping the complex machinery that underlies the Vatican as a whole. As we delve deeper into the chapters that follow, exploring the bank's role offers us a window into the Vatican's engagement with modern capitalism, ethical dilemmas, and political intricacies. The bank serves as a mirror reflecting both the divine aspirations and the earthly realities of the Vatican. It's a conundrum of faith and finance, holiness and worldliness, secrecy and revelation. And like many things associated with Vatican

City, the more you uncover, the more questions arise, enveloping the institution in a perpetual aura of mystery and fascination.

So, fasten your seatbelts—or perhaps your papal tiaras—as we journey into the labyrinthine world of the Vatican's financial heartbeat. It promises to be as enlightening as it is enigmatic.

2

Sacred Secrets: Delving into the Intricacies of the Vatican Bank

I n the modern lexicon of financial institutions, the Vatican Bank occupies a unique, almost mythic status. One imagines a scenario where divine revelations share the stage with financial statements, where the pursuit of holiness coexists with money transfers and where ethical dilemmas manifest not only in theological debates but also in portfolio management. This chapter delves into the intriguing yet often elusive dimensions of the Vatican Bank, exploring its underbelly of financial controversies and secrets. From allegations of money laundering to the enigma of hidden assets, this will be a journey through what may well be the world's most spiritually entangled financial institution.

The Godly and the Shadowy

Like any other bank, the Vatican Bank accepts deposits, transfers money, and manages investments. However, unlike other banks, it operates within the contours of an ecclesiastical state—the Vatican, an entity that claims to be guided by divine principles. This paradoxical situation becomes a fertile ground for ethical dilemmas. How can an institution that advocates spiritual values maintain its credibility while navigating the morally ambiguous waters of international finance?

The Layers of Secrecy

Adding another layer to its complex identity, the Vatican Bank is notoriously secretive about its operations. While some secrecy is attributable to protecting the financial contributions made for charitable causes, the lack of transparency often raises eyebrows. Over the years, the institution has been linked to a series of controversial affairs—some of which have included allegations of money laundering for organized crime syndicates, financing illicit arms deals, and even facilitating covert Cold War-era politics.

The Case of Money Laundering

Perhaps one of the most glaring controversies associated with the Vatican Bank is the specter of money laundering. In 2010, the bank faced a seismic tremor when Italian authorities seized €23 million from a Vatican account under suspicion of violating money laundering protocols. While the Vatican initially dismissed these charges as a "misunderstanding," the event ignited international scrutiny and spurred internal efforts to reform the bank's transparency standards.

Unveiling Hidden Assets

The rumors surrounding hidden assets within the Vatican Bank often sound like plots straight out of a Dan Brown novel. While it's hard to substantiate many of these claims due to the bank's elusive nature, questions remain. Where does the Vatican Bank invest its funds? Are there assets that have been strategically hidden from public scrutiny, perhaps to avoid the geopolitical ramifications of these investments? These questions loom large in any discussion about the bank's operations.

The Ambiguous Reforms

Amid mounting criticisms and regulatory pressures, the Vatican Bank has made a public show of reforming its operations to align more closely with international financial standards. Yet skeptics argue that these reforms are but superficial changes, strategically implemented to appease international critics while maintaining the core modus operandi. The opacity remains, fostering a culture of speculation and doubt.

Conclusion

The Vatican Bank, ensconced within a city-state that has spiritual influence over a billion souls, is a financial institution unlike any other. Its inner workings present a curious blend of sacred intent and profane complications. From laundering allegations to the clandestine world of hidden assets, the bank's activities generate both awe and suspicion.

The moral challenges the Vatican Bank faces serve as a microcosm of the larger ethical paradoxes that religious institutions often grapple with in a secular world. It's a divine comedy and tragedy, all rolled into one, residing in the complex interplay between the material and the spiritual. As we delve deeper into the other concealed aspects of the Vatican, this chapter serves as a financial prologue to the nuanced ethical and philosophical dialogues that await us. So, let's continue unraveling these sacred secrets, with eyes wide open but ever mindful of the mysteries that may never fully come to light.

3

Of Vaults and Virtues: Financial Records in the Secret Archives

I n the labyrinthine depths of the Vatican's Apostolic Palace, beyond the frescoes and corridors filled with history and art, lies a domain often relegated to the realm of legend: the Vatican's Secret Archives. Known officially as the Archivio Segreto Vaticano, it is a space most people only encounter through the lens of popular culture—a vault shrouded in as much mystery as the financial operations of the Vatican Bank. While the archives' most famous documents involve theological controversies, diplomatic cables, and historical events, less discussed are its financial records. In this chapter, we probe into this underexplored corner, asking what financial documents might be lurking within these hallowed halls, and why such records would be so stringently protected.

Scrolls and Ledgers: The Composition of the Archive

Although the contents of the Secret Archives are varied—ranging from Papal bulls and royal correspondence to ancient manuscripts—the existence of financial records is almost a certainty. Considering the Vatican's historical entanglements with empires, wars, and financial institutions, one could reasonably infer that the archives contain ledgers, transactional details, and perhaps even secret agreements that pertain to the Vatican Bank and other financial interests.

The Wall of Secrecy: Protecting What Exactly?

While the Vatican cites preservation of sensitive information as the reason for its secrecy, the mere speculation about what the financial documents might reveal raises important questions. Are these papers merely boring ledgers of routine transactions? Or do they contain information that could rock the foundations of the Church, such as undisclosed assets, shady deals, or financial misconduct? The very opacity of the archives feeds these questions and cultivates an atmosphere of mystique around Vatican finances.

The Role of Financial Records in Diplomacy and Politics

Money is never just about money, especially not when it comes to the Vatican. Financial assets can be strategically used or withheld for diplomatic leverage. Could the archives be holding key financial documents that have played a role in international diplomacy? Have secret deals been made in the name of peace or, conversely, war? The Vatican's role as a soft power in international relations could be deeply intertwined with its financial records.

Financial Ethics and Theological Implications

If one takes the Vatican's ethical teachings seriously, the existence of financial records in the secret archives raises profound theological questions. How can the Vatican reconcile its ostensible commitment to poverty and charity with the practical necessities of running what is, in effect, a global institution with vast financial needs and interests? The financial records could either exonerate the Vatican from various allegations it faces or deepen the ethical dilemmas it must navigate.

The Power and Pitfalls of Transparency

The broader question surrounding these hidden financial records is one of transparency. In an era where institutions are increasingly held accountable for their financial conduct, the Vatican's approach seems to be an anachronism, a relic from a time when religious institutions were beyond reproach. Yet, as demands grow for greater openness—not just from regulatory bodies, but also from the Catholic community—how long can the Vatican maintain its vault-like silence?

Conclusion

The financial records tucked away in the Vatican's Secret Archives are like Schrödinger's cat—both innocent and guilty until proven otherwise. Their existence in such a secretive space amplifies questions about the Church's financial ethics, its role in international diplomacy, and its commitment to transparency. As we pull back the veil on these records— or at least imagine doing so—we grapple with issues that strike at the heart of the Vatican's dual role as both a spiritual beacon and a temporal institution. These records, in their silent ambiguity, offer a potent critique of an institution navigating the delicate balance between earthly concerns and heavenly aspirations.

4

Economic Ethics: Where Finance and Morality Collide

In a world beset by economic inequality, environmental degradation, and social injustices, the concept of ethical finance has never been more relevant—or controversial. For the Vatican Bank, the gravity of this discourse is compounded by its association with an institution that stands as a moral authority for millions. This chapter delves into the economic ethics of the Vatican Bank, probing how its financial practices either contradict or align with Christian ethical standards.

The Economy of Salvation: Money and Christian Ethics

In Christian theology, money itself is not inherently evil. What matters is how it's used. Scripture advises against the love of money as the root of all evil, but it also speaks of wealth as a resource that can be used to help others. "What you did for one of the least of these brothers and sisters of mine, you did for me," says Matthew 25:40. These theological underpinnings present an intriguing backdrop against which to assess the Vatican Bank's activities.

Investment Dilemmas: The Case of Fossil Fuels and Arms

One of the most contentious issues in the realm of ethical finance is where a bank chooses to invest its money. Information on the Vatican Bank's investments is scarce, but the Church's teachings on stewardship of the Earth and peace would presumably bar investments in fossil fuels or arms manufacturers. Yet the opacity of the bank's operations makes it challenging to discern how closely these ethical guidelines are followed, leaving a gray area wide open for scrutiny and skepticism.

Charity Versus Profit: The Allocation Quandary

The Christian principle of charity is central to the ethical considerations of any financial operation associated with the Vatican. How much of the bank's income is directed towards charitable endeavors versus how much is reinvested for profit? The vagueness surrounding this crucial aspect of the bank's functioning raises essential questions about the application of Christian ethics in its financial decision-making.

Transparency: A Virtue or a Burden?

Christian ethics emphasizes the virtues of honesty and openness. However, the Vatican Bank's secrecy appears to be at odds with these principles. Critics argue that a lack of transparency enables corruption and undermines the Church's moral authority. In this context, the secretive nature of the bank's operations becomes more than a mere policy—it becomes an ethical quandary in itself.

Social Justice and the Vatican Bank

A core tenet of Christian ethics is the commitment to social justice, which calls for an equitable distribution of resources. How does the Vatican Bank contribute to this ethical obligation? Does it provide low-interest loans to disadvantaged communities, or does it prioritize investments that empower marginalized groups? Again, the lack of transparency hampers a comprehensive evaluation of the bank's performance in this area.

Conclusion

The Vatican Bank exists in a nexus where financial imperatives and ethical commitments engage in a complex dance. On one hand, it must manage its assets wisely to sustain the Church's vast operations; on the other, it must uphold a high moral standard that aligns with Christian ethics. This duality makes the Vatican Bank a compelling subject of inquiry, a microcosm of the broader tensions between finance and morality.

As we grapple with these ethical dilemmas, we must remember that the Vatican Bank is not just a financial institution but also a barometer of the Church's moral integrity. The challenge lies not merely in reconciling economics with ethics but in navigating the labyrinthine pathways where divine teachings and earthly necessities intersect, often in ways as intricate and enigmatic as a Renaissance tapestry.

Thus, as we move forward in this exploration, let us carry with us the perennial question: Can Mammon serve God? Or will the clash between financial pragmatism and ethical imperatives perpetually haunt the corridors of this unique institution? This is a story that demands more than just a balance sheet for its telling; it calls for a moral compass, one that points towards both Heaven and Earth.

5

The Economy of Salvation: How Money Flows Through the Vatican

The juxtaposition of economic pursuits and spiritual aspirations presents one of the most perplexing aspects of the Vatican's operations. Labeled by some as the "Economy of Salvation," this confluence of money and spirituality embodies the inherent paradox of a religious institution that also requires financial sustenance. This chapter scrutinizes the relationship between the Vatican's financial dealings and its religious missions, offering speculative insights into what the guarded Secret Archives might disclose about this complex interplay.

A Two-Way Street: Money and Mission

One cannot explore the Vatican's finances without touching upon its mission to propagate the Catholic faith. Indeed, it is this mission that justifies, to some extent, the collection of donations, the acquisition of assets, and even the operation of the Vatican Bank. Yet, how does money collected in the name of spirituality get channeled back into religious endeavors? This two-way street forms the cornerstone of the Economy of Salvation.

The Ethereal and the Material: Papal Projects

The money collected by the Vatican does not merely fill coffers; it fuels projects. These range from the obvious—such as building and maintaining churches, supporting clergy, and missionary work—to the less visible but equally significant efforts like education and social programs. What remains speculative but incredibly tantalizing is how these priorities might be detailed in the financial documents kept within the Secret Archives.

Between Heaven and Earth: Financial Reports as Moral Documents

If one were to gain access to the financial records stowed away in the Secret Archives, what ethical commitments would be unveiled? Do the spreadsheets align with sermons? Each line item is not just a monetary figure but an ethical choice, an articulation of what the Church deems worthy of investment. Thus, the financial archives can be viewed as moral documents, codifying in numbers the Church's ethical priorities.

Philanthropy or Folly: Questionable Investments

Even a cursory look at the publicized Vatican finances reveals investments and allocations that may appear perplexing or even questionable when juxtaposed against the Church's teachings. Be it investing in real estate ventures or stocks, the ways in which the Vatican places its bets can sometimes seem misaligned with its spiritual message. It provokes speculation about what other investments, perhaps riskier or even more controversial, might be lurking undisclosed within the Secret Archives.

The Dual Role of the Vatican Bank

As an institution that ostensibly exists to serve the mission of the Catholic Church, the Vatican Bank stands as a fascinating emblem of this economic-religious duality. The Bank's role isn't just to increase assets but also to channel funds into projects that resonate with Christian values. Could the Secret Archives hold evaluative documents that trace how effectively the Bank has been fulfilling this dual role over the years? The answer remains, for now, a matter of faith rather than fact.

Conclusion

The Economy of Salvation remains a subject enveloped in layers of devotion, duty, and dollars. The Vatican's financial mechanisms not only support its earthly operations but also underwrite its heavenly aspirations. However, the opacity surrounding these transactions invites a degree of skepticism, even cynicism, about whether financial actions genuinely mirror spiritual intentions. While we may never know for sure what the Secret Archives contain, the very act of questioning invites a form of enlightenment, forcing us to confront the uncomfortable yet essential questions that arise when we attempt to serve both God and Mammon in a world that demands allegiance to both.

6

Between Dogma and Reality: The Vatican's Ethical Dilemmas

The Vatican, standing as both a religious and a political entity, navigates a complex web of ethical decisions on a daily basis. While its public statements often advocate a specific set of moral and ethical guidelines based on Christian doctrine, the behind-the-scenes practices might tell a different story. This chapter scrutinizes the gap between the Vatican's public ethical stance and what internal documents, particularly those in the Secret Archives, could potentially reveal about its actual practices and beliefs.

The Public Persona: Moral Imperatives

From papal encyclicals to public addresses, the Vatican's ethical stance is well-documented and highly publicized. These communications discuss a wide range of issues, from the sanctity of life and social justice to the importance of environmental stewardship. But how do these ethical imperatives translate into daily decisions, especially financial ones?

Moral Accounting: The Hidden Ledger

Behind the gilded curtains, the Vatican operates like any other complex organization, juggling financial obligations and strategic priorities.

The Secret Archives might well contain documents that showcase the Church's moral reasoning when navigating these challenges. Could there be instances where ethical guidelines were bent or compromised for financial or political gain? If so, the impact on the Church's credibility would be enormous, opening a Pandora's Box of ethical quandaries.

Revisiting the Vatican Bank: Where Finance Meets Faith

The Vatican Bank, an institution shrouded in both reverence and mystery, serves as a focal point for this ethical tension. Publicly, the Bank claims to operate under Christian ethics, directing funds toward projects that are aligned with the Church's moral teachings. However, past allegations of corruption and financial misconduct raise questions about the alignment between public dogma and private dealings.

The Role of Investments: A Test of Principles

While Christian doctrine has much to say about the ethics of wealth, how the Vatican chooses to invest its assets remains a less transparent subject. Are these investments guided by the ethical principles proclaimed from the pulpit? Or do they prioritize financial gains over moral considerations? Hidden within the Secret Archives could be documents that clarify the Vatican's ethical calculus in its investment strategies.

Conflicting Partnerships: Diplomacy and Moral Trade-offs

The Vatican's diplomatic ties also present ethical complexities. As a sovereign entity, it maintains relationships with countries whose practices may contradict its publicly stated ethical stance. Might the Secret Archives contain diplomatic documents that shed light on how these conflicting partnerships are morally justified—or perhaps conveniently overlooked?

Conclusion

The tension between dogma and reality raises an array of ethical dilemmas that the Vatican must grapple with. While the Church's public persona advocates an uncompromising ethical framework, its internal operations may not always align with these standards. Should the veils of the Secret Archives ever lift, the revelations could either confirm the integrity of the Church's ethical stance or expose an institution in moral crisis. As we ponder this uneasy coexistence of ethics and operations, we are compelled to confront larger questions about the relationship between belief and practice—not just in religious institutions but in our own lives as well.

7

The Papal Vaults: What Lies in the Secret Archives?

Nestled within the intricate labyrinth of Vatican City lies one of the world's most enigmatic repositories—the Vatican Secret Archives. This chapter takes a speculative yet scholarly excursion into what might be stored in these vaults, emphasizing the historically significant documents that could lie within and scrutinizing the reasons behind their restricted access.

The Forbidden Library: An Overview

Contrary to the assumptions fueled by its name, the Vatican Secret Archives is not a subterranean lair brimming with nefarious secrets, but rather an extensive, largely unexamined collection of papal documents, state papers, correspondence, and other ephemera. Yet, its aura of mystique isn't entirely undeserved; the restricted access to the archives poses the question: What exactly is the Vatican preserving with such zeal?

Chronicles of Power: Treaties, Bulls, and Diplomacy

High on the list of anticipated contents are documents that have shaped the geopolitical landscape for centuries. Papal bulls, treaties, and diplomatic correspondence between world leaders and pontiffs could offer unique perspectives on key historical events. Are there unknown documents that could rewrite parts of history as we know it?

Heretical Texts and Trials: The Records of Apostasy

The archives might contain fascinating insights into the Vatican's stance on heresy and apostasy through the ages. Trial records, theological debates, and perhaps even communications regarding the infamous Inquisition could lie in the depths, waiting to be unearthed.

Divine Secrets: Mystical and Canonical Texts

Beyond the hard politics and grim trials, the archives could house invaluable religious and mystical texts. Could there be unreleased encyclicals, theological essays, or even accounts of mystical experiences that could deepen our understanding of Catholic spirituality?

Science and the Sacred: The Church and Intellectual Inquiry

The relationship between the Catholic Church and science has been fraught yet deeply intertwined. Might there be unknown letters or documents from luminaries such as Galileo, or lesser-known scientists and philosophers who challenged the Church's understanding of the world?

Forbidden Art and Censored Literature

Given the Vatican's historical role as both patron and censor of the arts, one can only speculate what creative works might be sequestered in the archives. Could there be lost works of art, forbidden books, or controversial writings that were considered too volatile for public consumption?

The Guardians of the Vault: The Select Few

Access to the archives is not merely restricted; it is a privilege afforded to a select few. What is the criteria for this exclusivity, and what does it reveal about the Vatican's priorities? Are there political considerations, or is the restriction merely a means of preserving the sanctity and integrity of the documents?

Conclusion

The Vatican Secret Archives, in their enigmatic seclusion, captivate the imagination with the promise of hidden knowledge and untold stories. As we probe the speculative edges of what might be contained within these sacred vaults, we must also ponder the ethical implications of restricted access to knowledge, particularly when that knowledge has the potential to reshape our understanding of history, spirituality, and even morality. In the end, the Secret Archives serve as both a literal and metaphorical space where the complexities of human knowledge, belief, and history converge in a tantalizing dance with the unknown.

8

The Librarians of God: Who Controls the Archives?

In the annals of history, gatekeepers of knowledge have wielded immense power. Whether it's the guardians of the Library of Alexandria or the modern arbiters of online information, those who control access to knowledge often dictate its interpretation and impact. But perhaps no gatekeepers hold more intriguing positions than those who supervise the Vatican Secret Archives. This chapter delves into the enigmatic individuals who hold the keys to this repository, examining how their roles may influence both the narrative and the perception of the Vatican.

The Hierophants: Roles and Responsibilities

We often imagine librarians as kindly individuals who help us find a good mystery novel on a rainy afternoon. But the stewards of the Vatican Secret Archives are not your everyday librarians. Tasked with safeguarding a plethora of documents that span over a millennium, these professionals operate more like security consultants than quiet custodians. What are their qualifications, and what responsibilities come with such an exalted position?

The Vetting Process: Who Gets Through the Gates?

The Vatican Secret Archives remain inaccessible to the general public, and only a select group of scholars are granted entry. The process of gaining approval for access is nothing short of Byzantine. How do these stewards of knowledge make their decisions? Are their criteria purely academic, or do political, religious, and social factors weigh into their judgments?

Curators of a Grand Narrative

Those who oversee the archives are not merely sentinels; they are also the curators of the Catholic Church's grand narrative. What they choose to make available for academic scrutiny shapes our understanding of religious history and the Vatican's role in it. Do these curators influence what aspects of Church history are studied, thereby creating a curated, sanitized history?

Echoes of Silence: What is Left Unsaid?

Inevitably, what remains off-limits to researchers speaks volumes. Could the gatekeepers be suppressing documents that might alter our perception of Vatican history? Whether by design or omission, the gaps in the historical record are as telling as the data that's available.

The Ethical Dilemma: Transparency vs. Sanctity

In most public libraries, transparency is the norm, but the Vatican Secret Archives operate on a different ethical plane. On the one hand, preserving the sanctity and integrity of the documents is a paramount concern. On the other, there's a moral imperative for transparency, particularly when the documents could illuminate dark chapters in Church history or reshape our understanding of global events. How do the archive's guardians navigate this ethical minefield?

The Modern Challenge: Digitization and Open Access

We live in an age where calls for transparency and open access to information have never been louder. How is the Vatican navigating the tricky waters of digitization and online access? Could modern technology force a change in the traditional ways of the Vatican librarians?

Conclusion

The figures who govern the Vatican Secret Archives are more than mere librarians; they are historians, ethicists, and, in some ways, political operatives. They wield an understated yet significant form of power that extends far beyond the marble walls of the Vatican. Their decisions on who gains access—and what remains hidden—shape not just historical research, but our broader understanding of one of the world's oldest continuous institutions. The questions surrounding their roles open a Pandora's box of ethical and epistemological dilemmas, pushing us to reconsider how knowledge itself is governed in the heart of the Catholic Church.

9

Documents, Scrolls, and Papal Bulls: What's Inside?

When envisioning the Vatican Secret Archives, one might conjure images reminiscent of the cavernous warehouse from the final scene of "Indiana Jones: Raiders of the Lost Ark." Rows upon rows of meticulously labeled manuscripts, ancient tomes bound in leather and vellum, and mysterious scrolls sealed with wax. This chapter aims to demystify what types of documents reside in these enigmatic vaults and why their contents are more than just relics—they are capsules of human history, ripe for exploration.

Manuscripts and Early Texts: The Dawn of Doctrine

One can imagine the archives housing ancient manuscripts that delve into the core tenets of Christian thought. These could range from early copies of the Gospels to obscure theological treatises that never made it into mainstream Christian doctrine. These texts offer us a glimpse into the evolution of Christian thought, a continuum that has undergone countless revisions, suppressions, and reawakenings.

Papal Bulls: Decrees that Shaped the World

Papal bulls, official papal letters sealed with a bulla, are among the most intriguing and consequential documents likely to be found in the archives. These range from mundane matters to pronouncements that changed the course of history. For instance, the "Dum Diversas" bull of 1452 sanctioned the Portuguese crown to conquer and enslave non-Christian populations, a decree with repercussions that ripple through history to this day.

Diplomatic Correspondence: A Window into Geopolitics

The Vatican has been a significant player on the world stage for centuries, and the archives must be a goldmine of diplomatic cables, treaties, and correspondence. These papers could reveal how popes brokered peace, instigated conflicts, or navigated the treacherous waters of international politics. It's not just a matter of antiquarian interest; these documents could offer fresh perspectives on old conflicts and current geopolitical tensions.

Canonical Laws and Decrees: The Rules of Heaven and Earth

The Vatican Archives likely contain the historical underpinnings of Canon Law—the internal regulations that govern the Church. Beyond theological implications, these laws have had a social and even political impact, shaping everything from marriage norms to legal frameworks in countries where the Church holds sway.

Inquisition Records: The Dark Side of Dogma

It's almost certain that the archives house records from the various Inquisitions conducted by the Church. These would include trial transcripts, verdicts, and perhaps even the Church's own internal debates over the ethics and methodologies of the Inquisition. Such documents offer a chilling yet invaluable window into how institutionalized religious fervor can tip into tyranny.

Secret Treatises and Forbidden Texts: The Controversial Collections

Rumors have long swirled about the Archives holding banned books or texts considered heretical. Though much of this is speculative, it is not entirely outside the realm of possibility. Given that the Church has, at various points, acted as both censor and protector of knowledge, it would not be surprising to find controversial texts tucked away in some remote corner.

27

10

Confessional Politics: LGBTQ+ Rights and the Church

The pulpit and the podium have often intersected, especially when it comes to issues of morality and human rights. But perhaps no issue has brought this intersection into sharper focus in recent times than LGBTQ+ rights. This chapter critically evaluates the Vatican's stance on this topic and speculates on what role this position might play in the contents of the secret archives.

The Catechism and Queerness: Doctrine Versus Reality

Officially, the Church's position, encapsulated in the Catechism, distinguishes between homosexual orientation—which it deems "objectively disordered"—and homosexual acts, which it considers sinful. This seemingly nuanced approach often leaves the Church at odds with itself, vacillating between pastoral care and doctrinal strictness. How might the archives contain documents that elaborate or further complicate this dichotomy?

Papal Positions: From Benedict to Francis

The stance of individual popes varies considerably when it comes to LGBTQ+ issues. Pope Benedict XVI was notably conservative, backing Church teachings that call homosexuality an "intrinsic moral evil."

Pope Francis, on the other hand, has adopted a more conciliatory tone, famously asking, "Who am I to judge?" What kind of internal memos, correspondences, or unpublished speeches might the archives hold that detail the evolving views of the papacy on this issue?

The Intersection of Secular Laws and Sacred Views

In many countries, LGBTQ+ rights have progressed substantially, prompting questions on how the Church grapples with these shifts in public opinion and legislation. Are there internal documents that discuss the Vatican's strategies for engagement with secular governments on this issue? If so, they would provide invaluable insights into the tension between religious dogma and evolving societal norms.

The Closeted Clergy: Silence and Scandal

The topic of LGBTQ+ priests remains a subject of intense debate and secrecy within the Vatican. The archives may contain records of internal discussions, psychological evaluations, and perhaps even confessions related to clergy who identify as LGBTQ+. The ethical implications of such documents would be a minefield, but their existence and what they reveal could be groundbreaking.

Marginalized Voices: Where Are the LGBTQ+ Theologians?

Theological contributions from LGBTQ+ perspectives have often been marginalized or outright silenced by the Church hierarchy. Could the Vatican archives hold unpublished works or correspondence from theologians who themselves were part of the LGBTQ+ community? Such materials could fundamentally alter our understanding of queer theology and its place within the broader spectrum of Catholic thought.

11

Silent Choirs: Where Are the Women?

The sanctified halls of the Vatican, echoing with centuries of prayer, debate, and intellectual pursuit, seem overwhelmingly male. Not just in its leadership or priesthood, but even in the stories told through its art and literature. This chapter delves into the place—or lack thereof—of women in the Vatican, and speculates on how this reality might be reflected in the Vatican's secret archives.

Behind the Marble and Gold: The Invisible Sisters

While women religious, nuns, and sisters contribute significantly to the Catholic Church's work worldwide, their representation within Vatican City is strikingly minimal. The archives could hold personnel records, papal correspondence, and policy documents that either explain or perpetuate this gender discrepancy. If absent, their lack becomes a silent but compelling commentary.

Canon Law and Canonical Exclusions

Canon Law, the internal legal system of the Catholic Church, rarely mentions women, and when it does, often in contexts that limit their roles and functions. Are there draft versions or historical iterations of these laws that offer more inclusive perspectives, or have women always been considered the "other" in these holy legal texts?

In Her Own Words: Female Saints and Theologians

From St. Teresa of Ávila to Hildegard of Bingen, women have contributed to the Church's spiritual and intellectual life. Are their writings, particularly those that deal with women's roles, adequately represented in the archives? And if so, are they being studied, promoted, and valued on par with their male counterparts?

The Maternal Image: Mother Mary and Beyond

The Virgin Mary occupies a special place in Catholic theology. Yet, the maternal archetype often does not translate into any real power or voice for women within Church hierarchies. Documents in the archives that explore or debate Marian doctrines could offer fascinating insights into how the Church negotiates the tension between veneration of the feminine and practical sidelining of women.

The Forbidden Discourse: Ordination and Leadership

One of the most controversial topics concerning women in the Church is their ordination as priests or deacons. Internal memorandums, theological evaluations, and even potentially secret studies could reside in the archives, documenting the Church's internal struggles with this issue. The repercussions of such documents, if they exist, would be monumental.

Sins of Omission: What's Missing Speaks Volumes

A telling feature of the archives could be what is missing: Are there gaps where the voices of women should be? Are the writings of female theologians conspicuously absent or underrepresented? These sins of omission can speak as loudly as any document, eloquently testifying to the silent choirs of women whose contributions have been systematically overlooked.

Conclusion

The story of women in the Vatican is less a tale told out loud than a narrative woven in hushed tones, tucked into the margins of grand historical accounts. What might exist in the Vatican's secret archives could provide a more nuanced understanding, breaking the seal on long-kept secrets and filling in the silent staves in the Church's largely male-composed hymn.

12

The Vatican: A Beacon and a Riddle

I n the heart of Rome, enveloped by the curve of the Tiber River, sits a walled enclave with a history so rich, its influence so vast, that it eclipses the dimensions of its mere 44 hectares. This is Vatican City—the smallest independent state in the world, but perhaps the most enigmatic. As the epicenter of Catholicism, it claims the devotion of more than a billion followers worldwide. The Vatican is not merely a place of worship; it is a formidable power structure, a cultural custodian, and a symbol of enduring mystery.

From the lofty spires of St. Peter's Basilica to the intricate frescoes of the Sistine Chapel, the Vatican embodies humanity's highest artistic and spiritual achievements. It has been the home to the brilliant and the divine—from Michelangelo to Pope John Paul II—each leaving an indelible mark on human history.

Yet, like any enduring edifice, the Vatican casts a long shadow. It is within this shadow that we must cast our gaze if we are to fully comprehend this multifaceted institution.

The Imperative of the Dark Exploration

No institution with over two millennia of history can evade the complexities and contradictions that come with wielding immense power. While the Vatican has been an incontestable force of good—advocating peace, preserving culture, and offering spiritual solace—it has also faced severe ethical quandaries, unsettling scandals, and a multitude of crises that challenge the very principles it vows to uphold.

Imagine the Vatican as a grand tapestry with gold and dark threads woven in intricate patterns. To appreciate only the gold threads—the canonizations, the charitable work, the artistic patronage—is to miss the texture of the whole. The darker threads—the inquisitions, the financial scandals, the struggles with modern ethical dilemmas—may be unsettling, yet they are just as integral to the complete picture.

By investigating the darker aspects of the Vatican's past and present, we not only seek accountability but also deepen our understanding of a highly complex institution caught between the divine and the earthly, the historical and the modern, the inspirational and the scandalous. It is through such a multi-dimensional lens that we can hope to grasp the Vatican in all its profundity.

In the chapters that follow, we will unravel these dark threads, tracing them back through the annals of history and into the complex weave of modernity. Welcome to a journey into the shadows over St. Peter's.

13

The Inquisition

The Holy Hammer: Introduction to the Inquisitions

The word 'Inquisition' often conjures images of dark dungeons, fiery pyres, and the relentless pursuit of heretics. These mental pictures are not mere dramatic exaggerations; they capture a grim but significant period in the Vatican's history. For an institution founded on the teachings of a man who urged his followers to "judge not," the Roman Catholic Church, as represented by the Vatican, found itself embroiled in not just one, but several inquisitions over the course of its history. The most infamous among these are the Roman and Spanish Inquisitions.

Roman Inquisition: When Rome Judged the World

The Roman Inquisition, also known as the Holy Office, was established in 1542 by Pope Paul III. Its primary objective was to combat Protestant heresy, but its reach expanded far beyond its original mandate. Heretical texts were identified and banned, scholars were summoned for questioning, and those deemed to hold heretical views were handed punishments ranging from excommunication to execution.

Spanish Inquisition: The Arm of the Church in Spain

Meanwhile, the Spanish Inquisition, sanctioned by Pope Sixtus IV in 1478 at the request of Ferdinand and Isabella, aimed to unify Spain under Catholicism. Unlike the Roman Inquisition, the Spanish variant was closely tied to the monarchy and, as such, bore a distinct political flavor. It not only persecuted Protestants but also Jews and Muslims, furthering the ambitions of a united and Catholic Spain.

Cultural Eclipse: Impact on Science and Culture

The inquisitions had a chilling effect on intellectual inquiry, especially during the Renaissance—a period synonymous with the rebirth of art, science, and humanistic values. The Vatican, once a patron of arts and sciences, found itself in a paradoxical position. It now stifled the very spirit of inquiry it had once nurtured. The Roman Index of Prohibited Books, which listed works that were forbidden to Catholics, included revolutionary scientific theories and groundbreaking works of literature and philosophy.

Case Study: Giordano Bruno—The Martyr for Infinity

Giordano Bruno was not merely a Dominican friar but a visionary who dared to dream beyond the horizon of established dogma. His beliefs in an infinite universe with multiple worlds directly contradicted the church's geocentric model. In 1600, he paid the ultimate price for his convictions, burned at the stake in Rome's Campo de' Fiori.

Case Study: Galileo Galilei—A Dialogue with Authority

Perhaps no other name encapsulates the tension between the Vatican and scientific progress as poignantly as that of Galileo Galilei. The genius who revolutionized astronomy found himself facing the Roman Inquisition in 1633. Although he recanted his heliocentric views under threat of torture, his work was added to the Index, and he spent the rest of his life under house arrest.

The Dual Legacy

The inquisitions left an indelible mark on the church's relationship with intellectual and cultural progress. While they led to a more homogenized doctrine, they also stifled scientific inquiry and fostered an environment of fear and self-censorship. The Vatican's role in these events raises uncomfortable but necessary questions about the ethical dimensions of its historical legacy.

These episodes serve as poignant reminders of what can happen when an institution wielding divine authority ventures into the treacherous waters of earthly governance. The Inquisition is not just a chapter in history; it's a lesson, a warning, and a call to vigilance.

Thus, our exploration into the Vatican's historical shadows begins. The Inquisition serves as our inaugural case study—an institution both feared and misunderstood, both an artifact of its time and a dark thread in the greater historical weave. What more remains in these historical shadows? The next chapters seek to illuminate further.

14

Political Intrigue and Papal Scandals

Introduction: The Thicker the Robes, The Deeper the Secrets

I f the papacy were a theater, then its stage has seen performances ranging from the saintly to the scandalous. The figure of the Pope, considered the Vicar of Christ on Earth, embodies a potent blend of spiritual authority and worldly influence. However, even divine theaters have their off-seasons, and the papacy has not been exempt from the all-too-human afflictions of corruption, greed, and political maneuvering.

Corrupt Popes: When The Seat of St. Peter Was For Sale

One name often muttered in the galleries of infamy is Alexander VI, born Rodrigo Borgia. His election to the papacy in 1492 marked not the advent of spiritual reformation, but a new pinnacle in papal corruption. Allegations of simony, or the buying and selling of church offices, swirled around him. His pontificate was a web of political machinations, including dubious alliances that served not the glory of God but the expansion of Borgia power.

But Alexander VI was hardly an anomaly. The history of the papacy offers a litany of popes who treated the Vatican more like a personal fiefdom than the epicenter of Christendom.

Nepotism and the Accumulation of Wealth: Keeping it in the Family

The term 'nepotism' originates from the Italian 'nipote,' which means nephew. Initially, Popes, who were theoretically committed to celibacy, would appoint their "nephews" to high-ranking church offices. In practice, these 'nephews' were often their illegitimate sons or other relatives. Over time, entire families such as the Borgias and the Medicis found themselves hoisted to prominence and wealth through church coffers. Such practices not only diluted the spiritual integrity of the church but also led to vast accumulations of wealth and property, often garnered from the faithful through tithes or the sale of indulgences.

The Excommunication Game: Holy Bans and Political Ambitions

Excommunication, the most severe form of canonical penalty, ostensibly serves as a mechanism for safeguarding the doctrinal purity of the church. However, history is replete with examples where excommunication served not theological precision but political expedience. Popes excommunicated emperors, kings, and even rival claimants to the papal throne, all in a bid to fortify their political clout. By wielding this spiritual cudgel, they blurred the lines between theology and political strategy.

The Clash of Two Kingdoms

The power dynamics between the Vatican and the world's temporal authorities have been as fluid as they have been fraught. When popes used their office to achieve personal or political gains, they ran afoul of the very scriptural teachings they vowed to uphold. The New Testament asks: "For what shall it profit a man, if he shall gain the whole world, but lose his soul?" It's a question that some popes, intoxicated by their own influence, seem to have overlooked.

15

World War II and Moral Ambiguity

In the Crucible of Conflict

Imagine the Pope's quarters as a quiet chamber where, even amidst the chaos of global warfare, a sense of divine serenity ought to prevail. Pope Pius XII, born Eugenio Maria Giuseppe Giovanni Pacelli, occupied this sanctum during a period where the world teetered on the brink of moral abyss: World War II. At times like these, the world turns its eyes towards spiritual leaders for moral guidance. Yet, what if those we gaze upon are themselves grappling with shadows?

The Delicate Dance: Pope Pius XII and the Axis Powers

Pius XII's papacy was enveloped in the dark clouds of World War II. The Vatican, technically a neutral state, had a treacherous tightrope to walk. On one side, the church's teachings stood firmly against the racial ideologies and authoritarianism espoused by Nazi Germany. On the other side, Rome was encircled by Fascist Italy, a key Axis power, and the Pope had to maintain a pragmatic relationship with Benito Mussolini's regime.

The Vatican's Diplomatic Quagmire

In 1933, the Vatican, then under Pope Pius XI, signed a concordat with Nazi Germany, aiming to protect the rights of Catholics under the Third Reich. Pius XII, then serving as Secretary of State for the Vatican, was instrumental in negotiating this agreement. While the concordat was initially intended to safeguard the church's interests, it later served as a propaganda tool for the Nazis, lending a semblance of moral legitimacy to a regime that would unleash unparalleled horrors.

Silence or Prudence? The Controversy Around the Holocaust

The most damning criticism aimed at Pius XII is his perceived silence during the Holocaust. Critics argue that the Pope, aware of the extermination of Jews, chose diplomatic caution over moral outrage. Proponents for Pius XII, however, contend that any public condemnation would have jeopardized the lives of even more Jews and Catholics behind enemy lines. They point to instances where the Pope discreetly aided Jewish refugees. This subject remains an ongoing area of research, debate, and, for many, deep emotional investment.

The Church's Wartime Dilemma

The Vatican's wartime conduct raises an unsettling question: How does a spiritual institution navigate a geopolitical landscape filled with landmines, both literal and ethical? At what point does prudence become complicity? And when does silence in the face of evil become a sin of omission?

An Incomplete Reckoning

Pius XII died in 1958, his legacy forever entangled in the barbed wire of World War II's ethical battlegrounds. Whether viewed as a cautious diplomat or a silent bystander, he serves as a complex symbol of the church's moral struggles during a dark epoch.

The Vatican's role during World War II remains one of the most contentious and hotly debated subjects in church history. It's a narrative punctuated with uncomfortable silences, unsettling alliances, and questions that perhaps have no satisfying answers.

By scrutinizing the Vatican's wartime conduct, we confront not just historical truths but also the very nature of moral leadership. In a world awash in shades of gray, the search for black-and-white answers is not just an intellectual exercise but a spiritual quest, one that each of us must undertake, guided by both heart and conscience.

16

1231: Establishment of the Papal Inquisition

The Papal Inquisition, established in 1231, was a pivotal event that would cast a long shadow over the history of the Catholic Church. Instituted by Pope Gregory IX, this tribunal was intended to combat heresy, a task that it undertook with zealous commitment. Operating under the logic that heretical views posed a threat to the Church and, by extension, the very fabric of Christian society, the Inquisition adopted methods that would today be seen as flagrant violations of human rights.

The establishment of the Papal Inquisition coincided with a period of immense social and religious upheaval. It was a time when various Christian sects were proliferating, and the Church viewed this heterodoxy as a challenge to its spiritual and temporal authority. The Inquisition was designed to assert this authority and to purify Christian communities of heretical influences.

While the primary focus was on theological purity, the consequences were starkly material. The Papal Inquisition became infamous for its use of torture to extract confessions, its confiscation of property from those deemed heretical, and its burnings at the stake, which were horrifying public spectacles meant to deter dissent. Many were subjected to these brutal methods, and the effects were felt beyond the individuals prosecuted. Whole communities lived in fear, and intellectual pursuits, particularly in fields like theology and science, were stifled.

45

17

1471: Foundation of the Vatican Library

The foundation of the Vatican Library in 1471 stands in stark contrast to the shadowy tales of inquisition and moral policing that are often associated with the Vatican's history. Established by Pope Sixtus IV, the library was a bold statement of the Church's commitment to knowledge, learning, and the preservation of ancient texts. At a time when the light of the Renaissance was starting to shine across Europe, the Vatican Library was envisioned as a repository of human intellect and a center for scholarship.

As the Renaissance began to pick up steam, so did the printing press and the appetite for knowledge. The revival of classical art, literature, and learning that characterized the period demanded a library to match its ambitions. In this context, the Vatican Library was more than just a collection of books—it was a powerhouse of intellectual activity that drew scholars, translators, and clerics from across Europe.

It wasn't just theological texts and biblical manuscripts that filled the shelves. The Vatican Library housed a wide array of knowledge, from Greek and Roman classics to early scientific manuscripts and maps of the then-known world. In essence, the library was a microcosm of the larger intellectual currents sweeping across Europe at the time. Its collections

46

were so diverse and rich that it later served as a foundation for studies in disciplines ranging from astronomy to zoology, offering a snapshot of human knowledge and ambition.

However, the library's very existence also prompts questions about the selective nature of knowledge preservation. For every text included, how many were omitted, lost, or deemed unworthy? To what extent did the Vatican Library contribute to the setting of a particular intellectual agenda, aligned with the Church's dogmas and belief systems?

Even as it facilitated the flourishing of intellectual pursuits, the Vatican Library also served as a stronghold of selective knowledge. Its establishment can be seen as a manifestation of soft power—informing, guiding, and sometimes limiting the boundaries of scholarly discourse. Still, one can't overlook its monumental contribution to human civilization—a sanctuary where wisdom from various corners of the Earth was collected, studied, and safeguarded for future generations.

18

1492-1503: Papacy of Alexander VI, known for nepotism and corruption

The papacy of Alexander VI, born Rodrigo Borgia, remains one of the most scandal-ridden and infamous periods in Vatican history. Serving from 1492 until his death in 1503, Alexander VI's reign was marred by allegations of corruption, nepotism, and moral depravity. In a historical context replete with ecclesiastical misconduct, his tenure often stands out as a high-water mark of papal indiscretions.

Let's explore the multiple facets of his papacy, each one casting a shadow that darkened the Vatican's image in ways still discussed today:

The Familial Web: Nepotism Incarnate

Alexander VI's nepotism was no subtle affair. He elevated multiple members of his family to positions of power, most notably his son Cesare Borgia and his daughter Lucrezia. Cesare, initially groomed for a career in the Church, would later become a fearsome military leader, while Lucrezia was used as a pawn in the marriage alliances that furthered her father's ambitions. The Borgia family's rise to prominence under Alexander VI was so intertwined with corruption and malfeasance that their name became synonymous with Machiavellian politics.

A Church for Sale: Simony and Indulgences

Alexander VI didn't just sell offices and titles; he commodified salvation itself. The selling of indulgences, effectively get-out-of-hell-free cards, reached a new level of audacity under his tenure. Simony, the act of buying or selling ecclesiastical favors and offices, was also rampant. It was as if the very sanctity of the Church was up for auction to the highest bidder.

Illicit Affairs and Scandalous Behavior

Alexander VI's sexual improprieties further tarnished the sanctity of the papal office. He fathered multiple children by his mistresses, a fact that he made little effort to conceal. The tales of lavish parties filled with hedonistic pursuits have been well-documented and serve as a testimony to his excesses.

Political Maneuvering: A Double-Edged Sword

Alexander VI was a cunning political operator. He sought to expand the Papal States and used his children to form alliances that would strengthen his power base. However, these actions often contradicted the spiritual mission of the Church, sowing discord among Christian states and setting the stage for the military conflicts that would mar his papacy and that of his successors.

19

1542: Roman Inquisition begins

The initiation of the Roman Inquisition in 1542 marked a significant and dark chapter in the annals of the Vatican and the broader Catholic Church. At a time when the Protestant Reformation was shaking the foundations of religious life in Europe, the Roman Inquisition represented a resolute, often ruthless, attempt to preserve the doctrinal integrity of the Catholic faith.

The Genesis: A Response to Protestantism

The Roman Inquisition was conceived as a mechanism to combat heresy, an urgent priority for the Catholic Church during a period of intense theological contestation. Martin Luther's 95 Theses had already sent seismic shocks through Europe's religious landscape, and the Roman Inquisition served as an institutional countermeasure to such transformative movements.

The Congregation of the Holy Office

Officially known as the Supreme Sacred Congregation of the Roman and Universal Inquisition, this body was responsible for maintaining and defending the integrity of the faith. With Pope Paul III's papal bull "Licet ab initio," the Congregation was officially instituted, and it was given sweeping powers to interrogate, prosecute, and deliver judgments on matters of heresy.

Tools of Fear: Torture and Execution

The Roman Inquisition was notorious for its use of torture to extract confessions. While it didn't introduce these methods—many were inherited from earlier inquisitions—it certainly employed them with a bureaucratic efficiency that made the process even more chilling. Executions, often by burning at the stake, served as public affirmations of the Inquisition's power and the Church's intolerance of heresy.

Impact on Science and Culture

The Roman Inquisition also had a stifling effect on intellectual life. Perhaps the most famous case was that of Galileo Galilei, who was tried and found guilty of heresy for his heliocentric model of the universe. His trial and subsequent house arrest sent a clear message to thinkers of the time: ideas that challenged Church doctrine, no matter how scientifically valid, were not just unwelcome but dangerous.

Legacy: A Complicated Moral Accounting

While the Roman Inquisition helped to preserve the unity of the Catholic Church in a period of potential fracturing, it did so at an enormous human and ethical cost. The methods employed tarnished the Church's moral standing, casting a shadow that persists in discussions of religious tolerance and freedom of thought. The Roman Inquisition was not merely a defense of the faith; it was also an assertion of ecclesiastical power, one that reverberated across the corridors of history, affecting lives and shaping the Church's complex relationship with dissent and reform for centuries to come.

20

1633: Trial of Galileo Galilei

The Skirmish Between Science and Doctrine: The Trial of Galileo Galilei

The year 1633 marks a pivotal moment in the tension between scientific inquiry and religious orthodoxy, crystallized in the trial of Galileo Galilei. This event was more than just a historical footnote; it became emblematic of the uneasy relationship between empirical evidence and established dogma, a tension that still reverberates in discussions about science and faith today.

A Revolutionary Gaze: The Telescope and the Heavens

Galileo's use of the telescope to observe celestial bodies provided groundbreaking insights that shook the very foundations of cosmology. He observed moons orbiting Jupiter, phases of Venus, and the rough, cratered surface of our own Moon—observations that were inconsistent with the Aristotelian and Ptolemaic views of a perfect, unchanging cosmos that had been endorsed by the Church.

Heresy on the Horizon: The Copernican Conflict

The real crux of the matter was Galileo's endorsement of the Coper-

53

nican heliocentric model, which posited that the Earth orbited the Sun, rather than the other way around. While Galileo didn't invent this model, his observations lent it significant credence. This directly contradicted the geocentric model supported by scriptural interpretations, setting the stage for an inevitable confrontation with the Church authorities.

The Roman Inquisition: A Stage Set for Trial

By the time Galileo was summoned to Rome in 1633, the Inquisition had already been a formidable arm of the Church for nearly a century. Known formally as the Congregation of the Holy Office, this body viewed itself as the guardian of orthodoxy, and it approached the Galileo case with the weight of that mission in mind.

Abjuration and Aftermath: The Silence of a Genius

After being found guilty of "vehement suspicion of heresy," Galileo was forced to recant his views publicly and spent the rest of his life under house arrest. His writings on the subject were placed on the Church's list of prohibited books, where they remained for centuries. This served as a chilling message to other scientists and intellectuals: challenge the Church's view of the universe at your peril.

Lasting Echoes: Science, Faith, and Freedom of Thought

The Galileo affair has since become a rallying point in debates about the freedom of thought and the relationship between science and religion. Though the Catholic Church formally removed the ban on Galileo's works in 1822 and cleared his name of heresy in 1992, the trial remains a symbol of the complexities and pitfalls that lie at the intersection of faith and reason.

21

1929: Lateran Treaty establishes the Vatican City as a sovereign state

From Temporal Power to Spiritual Statehood: The Lateran Treaty of 1929

The establishment of the Vatican City as a sovereign state in 1929 through the Lateran Treaty is a landmark event that not only reshaped the geography of Rome but also had a profound impact on the Catholic Church's role in world affairs. The treaty addressed the "Roman Question," a political and territorial dispute stemming from the 1870 annexation of the Papal States by the Kingdom of Italy, which left the Pope a "prisoner in the Vatican" for nearly six decades.

The Roman Question: A Historical Context

Following the unification of Italy in 1861, the Papal States, once a considerable temporal dominion under the Pope's rule, gradually shrank. By 1870, Rome was annexed into the Kingdom of Italy, leaving the Pope with only the Vatican and a sense of lost sovereignty. This led to an uneasy relationship between the Italian state and the papacy, a complex issue often referred to as the "Roman Question."

Mussolini's Ambitions: Politics Meets Religion

The 1929 Lateran Treaty was as much a product of political ambition as it was of spiritual necessity. Benito Mussolini, then Italy's Fascist leader, saw the treaty as a way to gain the Catholic Church's support, thereby legitimizing his regime. The Pope, on the other hand, was eager to regain a level of independence and sovereignty, even if it meant compromising with a dictatorial government.

The Provisions: A State Within a State

The Lateran Treaty comprised three parts: a political treaty recognizing the Vatican as an independent state, a financial convention providing the Holy See with compensation for its lost territories, and a concordat defining the religious and legal rights of the Church in Italy. For the first time since 1870, the Pope was a sovereign monarch, albeit of the world's smallest independent state.

Diplomacy and Divine Rights: The Vatican in the Global Arena

The Vatican City, though minuscule in size, has been monumental in influence. The Lateran Treaty allowed the Holy See to conduct diplomatic relations independently of Italy and play an increasingly important role in international affairs. It has since established diplomatic ties with almost every country in the world and has been a critical voice on matters of war, peace, and human rights.

Controversies and Criticisms: An Agreement Revisited

While the treaty resolved the Roman Question, it was not without its controversies. Critics argue that it lent legitimacy to Mussolini's Fascist regime. Subsequent popes and Italian governments have amended the concordat to address issues like religious education in public schools and the Church's tax-exempt status, highlighting the evolving nature of this historical agreement.

22

1933: Concordat with Nazi Germany

A Pact with Darkness: The 1933 Concordat with Nazi Germany

In 1933, the Vatican signed a Concordat with Adolf Hitler's Nazi Germany, a moment that has provoked intense scrutiny and moral questioning ever since. While the Vatican argued that the agreement was a pragmatic choice aimed at protecting the Church's rights in Germany, critics contend that it provided moral legitimacy to a regime that would soon commit some of the most heinous crimes in history.

The Tumultuous Background: Weimar Germany and the Rise of Hitler

The 1933 Concordat was signed in a Germany awash with political turmoil. The post-World War I Weimar Republic had been a period of fragile democracy, economic instability, and social upheaval. The Nazis, exploiting these conditions, came to power in January 1933. Hitler's ambitions for Germany were clear, and they included a complete overhaul of society according to his totalitarian and anti-Semitic views.

The Church's Dilemma: Protecting Its Flock

Faced with a hostile regime that had begun repressing Catholic organizations, schools, and publications, the Vatican believed a concordat would protect the rights of the Catholic Church in Germany. The Church's main concern was to maintain its ability to carry out religious duties and safeguard its property and organizations.

The Devil's Details: Terms and Outcomes

The concordat outlined several provisions aimed at preserving Church privileges, including the freedom to maintain religious schools and perform its liturgical functions. In return, the Church pledged to refrain from political activity—a term that was, unfortunately, subject to exploitation. Not long after the Concordat was signed, the Nazi regime escalated its anti-Semitic actions and moved toward military aggression, all while suppressing internal dissent, including from religious entities.

The Moral Quandary: Complicity or Naiveté?

Critics argue that the Concordat provided Hitler with a semblance of international legitimacy at a time when his regime was still consolidating power. They claim that the Church's diplomatic recognition inadvertently helped to stabilize the Nazi regime during its formative years. Defenders counter that the Vatican was in a difficult position and that the Concordat was a lesser evil aimed at protecting German Catholics.

Reckoning and Reflection: The Church's Ongoing Struggle

The Church has since expressed regret over some of its actions—or lack thereof—during this period. Pope John Paul II, for example, issued a public apology for the Church's failures to do more to combat the Holocaust. However, the Concordat remains a subject of ongoing debate among scholars, ethicists, and theologians.

23

1939-1958: Papacy of Pope Pius XII, controversial for his role during WWII

A Silence too Loud: The Controversial Papacy of Pope Pius XII (1939-1958)

The papacy of Pope Pius XII, which spanned the years 1939 to 1958, remains one of the most hotly debated periods in the annals of the Catholic Church. Situated during the cataclysmic events of World War II and its aftermath, Pope Pius XII has been at the center of debates about moral courage, complicity, and the ethical responsibilities of the Church during times of war and genocide.

Ascension to the Papal Throne Amidst Global Crisis

Pope Pius XII assumed the role of the spiritual leader of the Catholic Church at a moment of unprecedented global tension. Hitler had just invaded Poland, and Europe teetered on the brink of another world war. The Pope's initial messages seemed to convey a sense of neutrality, expressing a hope for peace but stopping short of condemning the aggression.

The Vatican's Diplomatic Tightrope

The Vatican, under Pius XII, claimed to follow a policy of neutrality during the war, attempting to be a mediator for peace. Yet, critics argue that this neutrality tilted dangerously toward appeasement, particularly concerning Nazi Germany and Fascist Italy. The Pope did maintain diplomatic relations with these regimes and never explicitly denounced the Holocaust.

The Holocaust: Silence or Prudence?

One of the most contentious aspects of Pope Pius XII's papacy is his silence during the Holocaust. Although there's evidence that the Vatican helped save some Jews from Nazi persecution, Pius XII never publicly denounced the mass extermination. The Church argues that a public denouncement could have worsened the situation, but critics claim that this inaction amounted to moral failure.

The Post-War Years: Shifting Focus to Communism

In the aftermath of World War II, Pope Pius XII shifted his focus towards the rising threat of communism. While he had been hesitant to explicitly criticize Nazi Germany, he had no such reservations about condemning communism, which he saw as a grave threat to the Church and to spiritual freedom. This shift has raised questions about the Church's priorities and moral consistency during Pius XII's reign.

Canonization Controversies: The Debate Continues

The debate over Pope Pius XII's wartime role resurfaced when the Vatican considered his canonization. Some argue that despite his controversial wartime conduct, his theological contributions and personal piety merit sainthood. Others vehemently disagree, stating that his failure to speak out against the Holocaust should disqualify him.

24

1981: Establishment of the Vatican Bank (IOR)

A Sanctified Vault? The Establishment and Controversies of the Vatican Bank (1981)

In 1981, amidst an era replete with economic expansion but also growing skepticism towards global financial systems, the Vatican took a decisive step to formalize its financial operations. Thus was born the Institute for the Works of Religion (IOR), commonly known as the Vatican Bank. Its establishment may have been a bureaucratic formality, but the institution soon became a nexus for intrigue, controversy, and questions about the very nature of morality in finance.

The Inception: Ideals and Realities

The Vatican Bank was ostensibly set up to manage the temporal goods of the Church and provide for its missions and charities. Yet from the outset, the IOR found itself entangled in a web of financial complexities that defied its holy intentions. Why did the Vatican, a religious entity, feel the need to establish a bank in the first place? Was it a pragmatic concession to modernity, or was there a deeper agenda?

A Mysterious Veil: The Bank's Unusual Status

One of the IOR's unique features is its extraterritorial status, granted by international agreements but also enshrouded in the secrecy characteristic of Vatican institutions. This status means that the bank operates in a regulatory gray zone, ostensibly to protect its religious mission but also inviting criticism that it provides a cloak for less-than-holy financial activities.

Scandals and Allegations: From Money Laundering to Organized Crime

Perhaps most notably, the Vatican Bank has been plagued by allegations of money laundering and connections to organized crime. One such infamous episode was the Banco Ambrosiano scandal, which led to the mysterious death of Roberto Calvi, known as "God's Banker." These scandals have not only damaged the bank's reputation but have also called into question the ethical standing of the Vatican itself.

Financial Reforms: A Path to Redemption?

In response to mounting criticism and scandals, the Vatican Bank has undergone several reforms aimed at increasing transparency and compliance with international financial regulations. This section will analyze these reforms and assess whether they are sufficient in not only restoring the bank's reputation but aligning its operations with the ethical standards expected of a religious institution.

An Ongoing Dilemma: Morality and Money

The Vatican Bank remains a fascinating study in contradictions—a religious institution entangled in worldly affairs, an entity that is both secretive and public, a symbol of both faith and fallibility. Its story compels us to reflect on the complicated relationship between morality and money, and it challenges us to question how institutions that profess the highest ethical standards can navigate the murky waters of global finance.

25

2002: Boston Globe's "Spotlight" investigation into sexual abuse in the Catholic Church

2002: Spotlight on the Darkness—The Boston Globe Exposes a Crisis in the Catholic Church

The year 2002 marked a seismic shift in public perception of the Catholic Church, thanks in large part to the Boston Globe's "Spotlight" investigation. This groundbreaking journalistic endeavor peeled back the veils of secrecy and silence that had long shrouded instances of sexual abuse within the Church. Not only did the report unearth heartbreaking stories of victims, it also exposed systemic failures that allowed such tragedies to occur and persist.

The Shockwaves: A Story Breaks

When the Boston Globe's investigative team published their first story on January 6, 2002, detailing allegations against John J. Geoghan, a former priest, it sent shockwaves through the Church and the world at large. The public was horrified not just by the scale and gravity of the abuse but also by the systemic cover-up perpetrated by the Church hierarchy.

The Domino Effect: From Boston to the World

The Boston case wasn't an isolated one. The Spotlight investigation had a domino effect, leading to revelations in dioceses across the United States and eventually around the world. Suddenly, the issue wasn't just about a few 'bad apples'; it was clear that the problem was systemic, reaching into the very foundations of the Church.

Journalism as Social Justice: The Impact of Spotlight

The team's work set a new standard for investigative journalism, leveraging legal documents, interviews, and indefatigable research to reveal a hidden world of suffering and systemic failure. It wasn't just a story; it was a form of social justice, shaking complacent systems out of their inertia.

The Church's Response: Admissions, Apologies, and Inadequacies

In the aftermath of the Spotlight revelations, the Church was forced to confront its failings publicly. Apologies were issued, and some steps were taken to address the crisis, but for many, the response was too little, too late. The investigation raised crucial questions about institutional responsibility, casting doubt on whether the Church could ever police itself adequately.

An Unfinished Story: The Legacy and the Lingering Questions

Nearly two decades have passed since the Spotlight investigation, but its impacts are still felt today. It changed the way we think about institutional abuse, forced transparency upon an unwilling organization, and empowered survivors to come forward, forever altering the power dynamics that enabled such abuse in the first place. Yet questions remain: Has the Church done enough to rectify its mistakes? Can it rebuild the trust that has been so profoundly damaged? And how do we reconcile the gravity of these sins with the potential for redemption?

The Boston Globe's Spotlight investigation didn't just write a story;

it revised the narrative of an ancient institution and forced an overdue reckoning with its darker angels.

65

2002: BOSTON GLOBE'S "SPOTLIGHT" INVESTIGATION INTO SEXUAL...

26

2010: The Vatican issues guidelines to prevent abuse

2010: A Long Overdue Response—The Vatican Issues Guidelines to Prevent Abuse

ADam Breaking: The Weight of Scandal

By 2010, the walls that had long protected the Catholic Church from full scrutiny were crumbling. With allegations of sexual abuse emerging globally, the Vatican could no longer afford to maintain its usual stance of denial or obfuscation. Public outrage and demands for action had reached a fever pitch. The world was watching, and the Church had to act.

A Framework Emerges: The 2010 Guidelines

In what was seen as a significant, albeit belated, move, the Vatican issued guidelines aimed at preventing further abuse within the Church. This document, circulated among all Catholic dioceses, established protocols for handling allegations of sexual abuse and sought to create a more transparent and accountable system.

Guidelines or Ground Rules? The Content Reviewed

The guidelines delineated key processes, including the obligation to report credible allegations of abuse to civil authorities—a step forward given the Church's history of internal handling. It also outlined procedures for the canonical trial of accused priests, aiming to bring some semblance of justice within the ecclesiastical framework.

Skeptical Reception: Too Little, Too Late?

While some lauded the Vatican for finally taking institutional steps to address the crisis, others questioned the efficacy and sincerity of these guidelines. Critics argued that without meaningful mechanisms for enforcement, these were but mere words on paper. The guidelines also stopped short of demanding the defrocking of priests convicted of abuse, a move many saw as a critical failure.

A Lens on Accountability: Loopholes and Limitations

The 2010 guidelines may have represented a step toward institutional reform, but they also highlighted significant gaps. For instance, they did not fully address the issue of accountability among the Church hierarchy—those who had turned a blind eye to the abuse or participated in cover-ups. This lack of comprehensive accountability measures remains a point of contention to this day.

A Start, Not an End: The Continuing Struggle for Reform

The Vatican's 2010 guidelines are best viewed as a chapter in an ongoing saga, not a conclusion. While they have provided a framework for addressing abuse allegations, they have not fully eradicated the systemic problems that allowed such abuse to flourish. Nevertheless, their introduction signaled a critical acknowledgment by the Vatican that change—imperfect and insufficient though it may be—had become unavoidable.

27

2013: Resignation of Pope Benedict XVI, the first pope to resign in 600 years

2013: A Break in Tradition—The Resignation of Pope Benedict XVI

A Papal Thunderbolt: The Resignation Heard Around the World On February 11, 2013, Pope Benedict XVI did something almost unthinkable in modern Catholic history: he resigned. The last pope to abdicate was Gregory XII in 1415, during the troubled times of the Western Schism. Benedict's decision shocked the global community, creating a ripple effect that challenged conventions and provoked a multitude of questions.

The Man Behind the Mitre: Who Was Pope Benedict XVI?

Before he was Pope Benedict XVI, he was Joseph Ratzinger, a conservative theologian known for his rigorous intellect. Elected in 2005, his papacy had been marked by efforts to reinforce conservative Catholic doctrine, often leading to polarizing debates on issues such as contraception, homosexuality, and the role of women in the Church.

"For the Good of the Church": The Reasons for Resignation

Benedict cited his deteriorating strength due to old age as the primary reason for his resignation. However, his papacy had not been without controversy, including criticisms for how he handled sexual abuse allegations. While no direct evidence links his decision to these scandals, the backdrop of crises undoubtedly cast a shadow over his reign and, potentially, his decision to step down.

A Changing of the Guard: The Election of Pope Francis

Benedict's resignation set the stage for the election of Pope Francis, a figure often seen as more progressive and more focused on social justice issues than his predecessor. The shift from a doctrinal purist like Benedict to a populist like Francis marked a dramatic change in the Church's focus, and many saw it as an opportunity for reform.

The Implications: A Precedent for Papal Resignation

Before 2013, the general assumption was that popes served until death, much like monarchs in days of old. Benedict's resignation shattered this age-old tradition, introducing the notion that the papacy could adapt to the personal and systemic challenges of modern times.

Revisiting the Role: Could This Happen Again?

By resigning, Benedict opened up a Pandora's box of questions regarding papal service and whether the role itself needs redefining. Some argue that this establishes a new paradigm that future popes may follow, especially if they find themselves unable to fulfill their duties due to health or other severe difficulties.

The resignation of Pope Benedict XVI stands as a watermark event in the long history of the Catholic Church. It wasn't merely the end of a papacy but a significant moment that signaled the Church's grappling with modernity, adaptability, and perhaps, its own vulnerabilities. In years to come, the Church will continue to wrestle with the complex implications of this ground-breaking event.

28

2018: Theodore McCarrick is removed from ministry following allegations of sexual abuse

2018: The Fall of a Cardinal—Theodore McCarrick and the Reckoning of the Catholic Church

The Unthinkable Unveiled: McCarrick Removed from Ministry On June 20, 2018, Theodore McCarrick, once the Archbishop of Washington and a cardinal of the Roman Catholic Church, was removed from public ministry following credible allegations of sexual abuse. This was a watershed moment in the Church's ongoing crisis, as McCarrick was one of the highest-ranking American figures in the Catholic Church to face such charges.

The Meteoric Rise: Who Was Theodore McCarrick?

Theodore McCarrick, born in 1930, climbed the ecclesiastical ladder with seeming grace and charisma. Known for his eloquence and fundraising abilities, he was a pivotal figure in American Catholic life, even advising presidents. But beneath this public image lay secrets that would eventually lead to his downfall.

From Accusations to Laicization: The Arc of Disgrace

Initially, McCarrick was accused of sexually abusing a minor decades earlier. Subsequent reports also revealed allegations of sexual misconduct with seminarians and priests. The Vatican conducted a canonical trial and found him guilty of sexual crimes against minors and adults, as well as abuse of power. In February 2019, he was laicized, meaning he was removed from clerical status.

The Network of Silence: Systemic Failures Revealed

The McCarrick scandal raised unsettling questions about how he could rise through the ranks despite rumors and even settlements related to sexual misconduct. His case spotlighted the inadequacies in the Church's systems for reporting and addressing abuse. It also hinted at a culture of complicity, where problematic behavior was either overlooked or deliberately concealed.

A Crisis of Faith and Credibility: Impacts on the Laity

McCarrick's fall from grace was more than just the failure of a man; it was a manifestation of the systemic issues plaguing the Church. For the laity, this was yet another rupture in their faith and trust in a religious institution that was supposed to offer moral guidance.

Shattered Illusions: The Road to Reform?

The McCarrick case accelerated ongoing conversations about reforms within the Church, especially concerning the handling of sexual abuse allegations. It resulted in renewed calls for transparency, lay involvement in investigations, and a more rigorous vetting process for clergy.

The removal and subsequent laicization of Theodore McCarrick marked a disturbing but necessary moment of reckoning for the Catholic Church. It served as a glaring illustration of the work that still needs to be done, fueling impassioned debates on how the Church can regain moral authority and safeguard against future abuses.

29

2020: Vatican releases report on McCarrick, admitting institutional failures

2020: A Moment of Reckoning—The Vatican's McCarrick Report Admits Institutional Failures

Breaking the Silence: The Vatican Speaks

On November 10, 2020, the Vatican took an unprecedented step by releasing a detailed, 461-page report on the rise and fall of Theodore McCarrick. This action punctuated the years-long struggle for transparency and accountability within the Catholic Church regarding issues of sexual abuse.

Confessions and Concessions: Admitting Institutional Failures

The report went beyond mere chronology and explored the systemic failures that allowed McCarrick's misconduct to go unchecked. For the first time, the Vatican admitted institutional and procedural errors, acknowledging that bishops, cardinals, and even Popes John Paul II and Benedict XVI failed to adequately address rumors and allegations against McCarrick.

The Role of Human Frailty: Misplaced Trust and Failed Oversight

A recurring theme in the report was the repeated willingness to give McCarrick the benefit of the doubt. Senior Church officials often relied on his own denials, bypassing formal investigations. The complexity of human error and misjudgment was laid bare, illustrating how individual shortcomings can catalyze systemic failure.

A Wake-Up Call: Redefining Protocols and Policies

The revelations ignited fresh debates on the efficacy of the Church's existing protocols for reporting and investigating sexual abuse. The Church could no longer evade the urgency for sweeping reforms, including robust background checks, clear channels for reporting abuse, and protocols to ensure objective, thorough investigations.

A Stir among the Faithful: Community Reactions

The McCarrick report sent shockwaves through the global Catholic community, shaking the trust of many. Yet, for some, the Vatican's unprecedented transparency was seen as a step—albeit belated—toward cleansing the institution of its deep-seated issues.

Rebuilding the Rubble: What Comes Next?

The McCarrick report didn't offer a neat resolution but rather intensified the clamor for meaningful change. Its sobering admissions now serve as the Church's uncomfortable but necessary testament, a historic document against which future reforms will be measured.

The release of the 2020 McCarrick report marked an inflection point in the Church's ongoing journey towards redemption and reform. Although it laid bare disturbing instances of institutional failure, it also signaled a potential turning point in the Church's commitment to transparency, accountability, and safeguarding the vulnerable—a milestone in the ongoing quest for atonement and institutional soul-searching.

30

Pope Alexander VI (Rodrigo Borgia): The Infamous Renaissance Pontiff

arly Life and Ascent to the Papacy

- Born Rodrigo Borgia in 1431 in the Kingdom of Valencia, Spain.
- Came from a prominent and wealthy family that played a significant role in his early career in the Church.
- Became a cardinal in 1456 and later was elected as Pope in 1492, taking the name Alexander VI.

Pontificate and Controversies

- Alexander VI's papacy was marked by controversies and scandals that would earn him a notorious place in history.
- Known for his pursuit of power, wealth, and political influence, often at the expense of moral and ethical considerations.
- Elevated several of his family members to high positions within the Church and secular governments, practicing nepotism on a grand scale.

- His son Cesare Borgia became infamous for his ruthless political ambitions and military campaigns.
- The Borgia family's extravagant lifestyle, lavish parties, and alleged immoral behavior contributed to their notoriety.

Legacy and Historical Assessment

- Pope Alexander VI's legacy is one of moral ambiguity and scandal.
- Despite his controversial personal life and political maneuverings, he made significant administrative contributions to the Church, including reforming the papal bureaucracy.
- His papacy serves as a cautionary tale about the potential dangers of unchecked power and the compromises that can come with it.
- Alexander VI's reign remains a point of fascination and discussion in the context of Renaissance papal history.

31

Galileo Galilei: The Renowned Scientist and the Roman Inquisition

Early *Life and Scientific Contributions*

- Born on February 15, 1564, in Pisa, Italy.
- A polymath who made groundbreaking contributions to physics, astronomy, mathematics, and philosophy.
- Known for his development of the telescope, which he used to make groundbreaking astronomical observations.

Heliocentric Views and Conflict with the Church

- Galileo's most famous contribution was his support of the helio-centric model, which proposed that the Earth revolved around the Sun.
- His heliocentric views challenged the geocentric model supported by the Catholic Church, which held that the Earth was at the center of the universe.
- In 1616, the Roman Catholic Church's Congregation of the Index declared heliocentrism as formally heretical, and Galileo was for-

bidden to teach or defend it.

Trial and Conviction

- In 1632, Galileo published his book "Dialogue Concerning the Two Chief World Systems," which defended heliocentrism and criticized the geocentric model.
- This led to his summons to Rome to stand trial before the Roman Inquisition in 1633.
- Under the threat of torture, Galileo was forced to recant his heliocentric views and was found guilty of heresy.
- He spent the rest of his life under house arrest in Florence, Italy.

Legacy

- Galileo's trial and conviction have been seen as a symbol of the conflict between science and religion, though the relationship between the two has evolved over time.
- His work laid the foundation for modern observational astronomy and the scientific method.
- Galileo's courage in defending his scientific beliefs has made him a symbol of scientific integrity and the pursuit of knowledge.

32

Pope Pius XII (Eugenio Pacelli): Controversial Papacy during WWII and the Holocaust

arly Life and Papal Ascension

E
- Born Eugenio Pacelli on March 2, 1876, in Rome, Italy.
- Ordained as a priest in 1899, Pacelli pursued a diplomatic career within the Vatican's diplomatic corps.
- Elected as Pope Pius XII on March 2, 1939, just before the outbreak of World War II.

Papacy during World War II

- Pope Pius XII's papacy coincided with one of the darkest periods in human history, World War II.
- Faced with the horrors of the Holocaust and widespread suffering, his papacy was marked by complex moral and political challenges.

Controversies and Criticisms

- Pius XII has been a subject of controversy and debate for his perceived lack of strong public condemnation of the Holocaust.

- Some critics argue that he did not do enough to intervene or publicly denounce the mass murder of Jews and other persecuted groups.
- Others contend that he worked behind the scenes to help rescue Jews and supported efforts to provide aid and assistance.

Debates over His Legacy

- The controversy surrounding Pius XII's wartime actions or inactions remains a topic of intense debate among historians and scholars.
- Some argue that his papacy was characterized by a cautious and diplomatic approach to protect Catholics in Nazi-occupied territories.
- Others assert that his response to the Holocaust was inadequate given the magnitude of the atrocities.

Posthumous Recognition and Ongoing Discussions

- After his death in 1958, Pius XII's actions during World War II have been a subject of ongoing evaluation.
- The Vatican's archives on his papacy were opened for research in 2020, shedding new light on his actions and decisions during this critical period.
- Pope Pius XII's legacy continues to be a matter of historical analysis, moral inquiry, and debate regarding the role of religious leaders during times of great moral crisis.

33

Cardinal Bernard Law: The Scandal and Resignation in Boston

arly Life and Ecclesiastical Career

- Born on November 4, 1931, in Torreon, Mexico, Bernard Francis Law was ordained as a priest in 1961.
- He held various positions within the Catholic Church and served as Bishop of Springfield–Cape Girardeau, Missouri, before becoming Archbishop of Boston in 1984.

The "Spotlight" Investigation and Scandal

- In 2002, the Boston Globe's "Spotlight" investigative team exposed the widespread sexual abuse of children by Catholic priests in the Archdiocese of Boston.
- The investigative reporting revealed not only the extent of the abuse but also the Church's efforts to cover up and protect abusive priests.
- Cardinal Law's role in the scandal became a focal point. It was revealed that he had reassigned known abusive priests to new parishes rather than reporting them to authorities or removing them

80

from ministry.

Resignation

- The public outcry following the "Spotlight" investigation led to widespread calls for Cardinal Law's resignation.
- On December 13, 2002, Pope John Paul II accepted Law's resignation as Archbishop of Boston.
- This marked a significant moment in the Church's history, as it highlighted the gravity of the sexual abuse crisis and the need for accountability.

Later Life and Death

- After his resignation, Cardinal Law was reassigned to the Vatican, where he held various positions.
- He continued to face criticism and was seen by many as a symbol of the Church's mishandling of the abuse crisis.
- Cardinal Bernard Law passed away on December 20, 2017, in Rome, Italy.

Legacy and Impact

- Cardinal Law's role in the Boston sexual abuse scandal remains a dark chapter in the history of the Catholic Church in the United States.
- The scandal prompted a reckoning within the Church, leading to increased efforts to address clergy abuse and provide support to survivors.
- Cardinal Law's resignation was a significant moment in the broader global conversation about accountability, transparency, and the

protection of children within the Church.

34

Theodore McCarrick: The Disgraced American Cardinal

arly Life and Ecclesiastical Career

- Born on July 7, 1930, in New York City, Theodore Edgar McCarrick entered the priesthood and was ordained in 1958.
- His ecclesiastical career saw him rise through the ranks, and he became a cardinal in 2001, holding a prominent position within the American Catholic Church.

Allegations and Investigations

- In 2018, allegations of sexual misconduct involving McCarrick began to surface publicly.
- These allegations included sexual abuse of minors and seminarians and had reportedly occurred over several decades.
- The revelations sent shockwaves through the Catholic Church in the United States and beyond.

Defrocking and Ongoing Fallout

- Following investigations and mounting evidence, Theodore McCarrick was found guilty by the Vatican in 2019.
- He was subsequently laicized, or defrocked, a rare and severe punishment that removed him from the priesthood.
- McCarrick's defrocking marked a significant moment in the Church's response to allegations of sexual abuse, as it demonstrated a willingness to hold even high-ranking clergy accountable.

Impact and Reckoning

- The case of Theodore McCarrick added to the growing scrutiny and criticism of how the Catholic Church had handled allegations of sexual abuse by clergy.
- It also contributed to discussions about the need for greater transparency, accountability, and safeguarding measures within the Church.
- Survivors of abuse, advocacy groups, and many Catholics demanded systemic changes to prevent such abuses from occurring in the future.

Theodore McCarrick's downfall serves as a stark reminder of the gravity of sexual abuse within the Church and the urgent need for reform. It also underscored the willingness of the Vatican to take unprecedented steps to address allegations of misconduct, even at the highest levels of the hierarchy.

35

Marcial Maciel: Founder of the Legion of Christ and Scandal-Plagued Leader

arly Life and the Legion of Christ

E
- Marcial Maciel Degollado was born on March 10, 1920, in Cotija, Mexico.
- He founded the religious congregation known as the Legion of Christ in 1941, with the aim of training priests and spreading Catholicism.

Initial Success and Influence

- Under Maciel's leadership, the Legion of Christ expanded rapidly and gained significant influence within the Catholic Church.
- The organization established seminaries, schools, and universities around the world, attracting many young men to the priesthood and religious life.

Allegations of Abuse and Misconduct

- Beginning in the 1990s, allegations of sexual abuse and misconduct by Maciel began to surface.
- Accusers included former members of the Legion of Christ who claimed they had been abused by Maciel during their time in the congregation.
- Maciel faced numerous accusations of sexually abusing minors, including seminarians, over several decades.

Vatican Investigation and Consequences

- Despite initial resistance, the Vatican launched an investigation into the allegations against Maciel.
- In 2006, the Vatican announced that Maciel had been found guilty of "seriously and objectively immoral behavior" and was instructed to lead a life of "prayer and penance."
- He was effectively removed from public ministry, and restrictions were placed on his activities.

Impact on the Legion of Christ

- The revelations surrounding Maciel had a profound impact on the Legion of Christ.
- It led to a period of internal reform and soul-searching within the congregation.
- The Legion faced the challenge of addressing its founder's tarnished legacy while continuing its mission.

Marcial Maciel's story is a stark example of the harm that can occur when allegations of abuse are ignored or concealed within religious organizations. It also highlights the importance of accountability and transparency within religious institutions and the broader conversations

about safeguarding vulnerable individuals within religious communities.

87

36

Countless Cases

The Case of Father John Geoghan - A central figure in the Boston abuse scandal

John Geoghan, ordained in 1962, was shuffled from parish to parish despite allegations of sexual abuse going back to at least the 1970s. A central figure in the Boston Globe's 2002 "Spotlight" investigation, Geoghan was eventually convicted of indecent assault and battery in 2002 for groping a 10-year-old boy. However, it is believed that he molested nearly 150 children over three decades. Geoghan was sentenced to a nine-to-ten-year prison term but was murdered by a fellow inmate in 2003.

The Case of Father Paul Shanley - Another key figure in the Boston scandal

Paul Shanley was a charismatic priest known for his work with troubled youth, but his legacy turned out to be anything but laudable. Accusations against Shanley also emerged from the "Spotlight" investigation, revealing his history of sexually abusing minors. Disturbingly, some of these acts took place during so-called "counseling sessions." Shanley was defrocked in 2004 and convicted in 2005 on charges of raping a child. He was sentenced to 12 to 15 years in prison and was released on parole in 2017 after serving 12 years.

Archbishop Theodore McCarrick (2018) – Removed from ministry following allegations

Theodore McCarrick, once a prominent Archbishop of Washington, D.C., and a cardinal, was removed from public ministry in 2018 after credible allegations of sexual abuse surfaced. The allegations ranged from misconduct with adult seminarians to the sexual abuse of minors. McCarrick was eventually laicized by Pope Francis in February 2019, a move considered to be the final step in stripping him of his clerical status and one of the highest-profile downfalls in the Catholic Church's history. The Vatican's subsequent report in 2020 admitted to systemic failings in handling the McCarrick case, extending back several papacies.

The Case of Marcial Maciel – Founder of the Legion of Christ, accused of abuse

Marcial Maciel, a Mexican priest, founded the Legion of Christ, a Roman Catholic congregation of priests. Maciel was a favored figure in Vatican circles, particularly during Pope John Paul II's papacy. However, allegations against him emerged, including sexual abuse of minors, drug abuse, and even fathering children. It wasn't until 2006, when Pope Benedict XVI ordered him to retire to a life of "prayer and penitence," that Maciel faced any form of reprimand. He died in 2008, without facing any legal repercussions, leaving behind a religious order struggling with the dark legacy of its founder.

Both cases exemplify the church's systemic struggles with issues of accountability and transparency. While the ecclesiastical repercussions were significant, especially in McCarrick's case, the institutional mechanisms that allowed these men to commit such acts for years, if not decades, highlight the urgency for more profound reforms.

The Pennsylvania Grand Jury Report (2018) - Found credible allegations against over 300 priests.

The Pennsylvania Grand Jury Report, released in August 2018, was a seismic moment in the ongoing narrative of sexual abuse within the Catholic Church. The report identified credible allegations against over 300 priests across six dioceses in Pennsylvania, affecting more than 1,000 child victims. The detailed, 1,400-page report laid bare a "systematic" cover-up by church leaders over seven decades.

One of the most disturbing elements of the report was the revelation that senior church officials not only failed to act but participated in obfuscation, victim-blaming, and shuffling offending priests from parish to parish, thereby perpetuating the cycle of abuse. Although the grand jury report could only lead to a limited number of new prosecutions due to statutes of limitations, it nevertheless ignited a national conversation about accountability and prompted other states to launch similar investigations.

What makes this case stand out is its sheer scope—hundreds of priests, a comprehensive cover-up, and a staggering number of victims. In the public consciousness, it marked a tipping point, substantially eroding the moral authority of the Catholic Church in the United States and forcing both secular and ecclesiastical authorities to reevaluate their approach to justice and reparation in the face of clerical sexual abuse.

The Case of Cardinal George Pell (Australia) - High-ranking Vatican official charged with sexual abuse.

Cardinal George Pell, once among the Vatican's most powerful officials, became a symbol of the church's convoluted handling of sexual abuse allegations when he was convicted in Australia in 2018. The cardinal faced multiple counts of sexual abuse against choirboys in the 1990s when he was Archbishop of Melbourne. His conviction sent shockwaves through the Catholic community worldwide, not just for the crimes themselves but because of Pell's high standing within the Vatican—he had served as the Vatican's treasurer, making him one of the highest-ranking church officials to face such allegations.

In a twist of events, Pell's conviction was overturned by the High Court of Australia in April 2020, citing insufficient evidence to sustain the guilty verdict. The acquittal was met with mixed reactions. Supporters saw it as a vindication, while critics questioned whether high-ranking officials within the Church are truly held accountable for their actions.

The Cardinal Pell case draws attention to the global dimension of the Church's abuse scandal, spotlighting how even the upper echelons of the Vatican are not immune. While Pell was ultimately acquitted, the very fact that he faced trial represents a significant shift in how allegations against high-ranking church officials are treated. The case adds another layer of complexity to the ongoing discourse around accountability, as it demonstrates both the possibilities and limitations of legal systems in grappling with decades or even centuries of institutional abuse.

Murphy Report (Ireland) - Investigated Allegations in the Archdiocese of Dublin

In 2009, the Irish government published the Murphy Report, a shocking and comprehensive investigation into child sexual abuse allegations involving clergy in the Archdiocese of Dublin. Spanning a period from 1975 to 2004, the report scrutinized the actions of over 300 priests, with 46 cases examined in considerable detail. The impact was seismic, both within Ireland—a nation where Catholicism is deeply woven into the cultural and moral fabric—and beyond.

What made the Murphy Report stand out was its damning indictment of both individual wrongdoers and the Church as an institution. It accused Church authorities of covering up abuse and enabling the predators to continue their horrific acts, often merely transferring them to other parishes where they could find new victims. The focus was not just on the individual perpetrators but on a pervasive culture of secrecy and denial.

The release of the Murphy Report sent ripples through the Catholic world, triggering similar investigations in other countries and opening up a broader conversation on how systemic abuse could be. It highlighted the urgent need for transparency, accountability, and reform, pressing issues that the Church continues to grapple with today.

Although some clerics were eventually defrocked or faced legal consequences, many have criticized the aftermath as insufficient, given the scale of the suffering. Some of the accused priests were sheltered by the Church, and many victims felt that justice was not fully served. Nonetheless, the Murphy Report stands as a watershed moment in the ongoing struggle to bring accountability to an institution often cloaked in secrecy and tradition.

Cloyne Report (Ireland) - Examining the Diocese of Cloyne's Response to Allegations

The Cloyne Report, released in 2011, served as another grim chapter in Ireland's confrontation with the issue of sexual abuse within the Catholic Church. Focusing on the Diocese of Cloyne, the report examined how allegations against 19 clerics were handled from 1996 to 2009. Unlike the Murphy Report, which was released two years prior, the Cloyne Report drilled down on a more localized scale but was no less damning in its findings.

The report concluded that Bishop John Magee and others in the Church hierarchy had not only failed to report allegations but had also mishandled the Church's own internal inquiries. In some cases, this had the unfortunate consequence of leaving the alleged perpetrators in positions where they continued to be a risk to children. The Cloyne Report was damning in its critique, highlighting significant failures in the Church's own established procedures—procedures which were meant to be a roadmap for dealing with such grave allegations.

Perhaps most shockingly, the Cloyne Report revealed that even as late as 2008—more than a decade after the Church in Ireland instituted reforms to handle abuse claims—key officials were still disregarding those guidelines. This highlighted a profound issue: the disconnect between public statements and internal practices.

The fallout from the Cloyne Report was immediate and intense, leading to the resignation of Bishop Magee and plunging the Catholic Church in Ireland into a new crisis of confidence. The Vatican was forced to recall its ambassador to Ireland for consultations, and even the then-Irish Prime Minister Enda Kenny felt compelled to issue a scathing critique of the Church's conduct.

While the Cloyne Report did lead to some disciplinary actions and legal proceedings, it also bolstered the argument that systemic change was needed—not just in Ireland but across the entire global network of the Catholic Church. The report remains a grim testament to the challenges that lie ahead in ensuring that the Church is a place of safety and sanctity for all.

The Case of Cardinal Bernard Law - The Fall of a Powerful Figure Amid Scandal

Cardinal Bernard Law, who was Archbishop of Boston from 1984 to 2002, became one of the most high-profile casualties of the Church's sexual abuse scandal. A powerful and influential figure not just in Boston but in the global Catholic hierarchy, Law's downfall came after revelations that he had systematically covered up sexual abuse allegations against priests in his archdiocese.

His tenure came under intense scrutiny following the Boston Globe's "Spotlight" investigation, which unearthed evidence of a large-scale, systemic problem involving the sexual abuse of minors by clergy and the subsequent cover-up by Church officials. While Cardinal Law was not directly accused of abuse, he was found to have reassigned priests who were known abusers to new parishes rather than reporting them to law enforcement or removing them from ministry.

The crisis reached a tipping point in 2002 when internal Church documents revealed just how much Cardinal Law and his subordinates had known about the scale of abuse, and how little they had done to address it. Public outrage was swift and severe, and Law became the focal point of demonstrations and calls for accountability.

Facing mounting pressure, Cardinal Law resigned from his position in Boston in December 2002, an almost unprecedented step for a figure of his stature. However, his resignation did not translate to a total fall from grace within the Vatican's walls. In 2004, he was appointed Archpriest of the Basilica di Santa Maria Maggiore in Rome, a position he held until his retirement in 2011. He passed away in 2017.

The case of Cardinal Bernard Law is often cited as emblematic of the Church's wider failure to address the sexual abuse crisis effectively. It exposed a culture of silence and self-protection that permeated the highest levels of the Church's hierarchy, thereby raising uncomfortable questions about institutional complicity. It also served as a catalyst for lay Catholics, activists, and lawmakers to demand sweeping changes in how the Church handled allegations of abuse, with varying degrees of success.

The Case of Father Lawrence Murphy - A Haunting Legacy in Wisconsin

Father Lawrence Murphy's name became synonymous with one of the most egregious instances of sexual abuse within the Catholic Church in the United States. He served at the St. John's School for the Deaf in St. Francis, Wisconsin, from 1950 until 1974. Murphy was fluent in American Sign Language, and he was initially well-regarded for his work with deaf children. However, he took advantage of his position and the vulnerability of his students to commit widespread sexual abuse.

Estimates suggest that he may have molested up to 200 boys during his tenure at the school.

Murphy was moved to different parishes following complaints but was never defrocked or officially disciplined by the Church. Several bishops and other church officials were allegedly aware of Murphy's actions but chose to move him to new assignments rather than remove him from ministry entirely. Some of the victims assert that they tried to alert Church authorities but were met with skepticism and inaction.

The case gained renewed attention in the early 2000s when documents were released showing that several decades prior, the Vatican had been made aware of the allegations against Murphy but had not taken action to remove him or report him to the civil authorities. The revelations stirred outrage, especially given that Murphy was allowed to retire in good standing in 1993 and lived freely until his death in 1998. No criminal charges were ever filed against him.

The case of Father Lawrence Murphy is especially haunting due to the systemic failures it illuminated. Here was a man who exploited his position of trust to commit horrific abuses against some of the most vulnerable members of society. Even more disheartening was the institutional inertia that appeared to prioritize the Church's reputation over the safety and well-being of its congregants. Murphy's story is a sorrowful testament to the urgent need for radical reforms within the Church to address issues of sexual abuse and accountability.

The Case of Bishop Robert Finn - A Landmark for Episcopal Accountability

In the annals of sexual abuse scandals within the Catholic Church, the case of Bishop Robert Finn stands out for a unique reason: it was the first time a Catholic bishop in the United States was held criminally accountable for failing to report child abuse. Appointed the bishop of the Diocese of Kansas City-St. Joseph in Missouri in 2005, Finn was later convicted in 2012 for not alerting authorities about a priest, Father Shawn Ratigan, who had taken lewd photographs of young girls in his parish.

While Father Ratigan was the immediate perpetrator, it was Bishop Finn's dereliction of duty that made headlines. When concerns were first raised about Ratigan's behavior, Finn had ample opportunity to report the situation to civil authorities. Church officials had discovered the troubling images on Ratigan's laptop in December 2010 but did not turn them over to police until May 2011, and that too, only after Ratigan had attempted suicide. During this time, Ratigan was allowed to attend events with children and even preside over a girl's First Communion ceremony.

For his failure to act promptly, Finn was charged with a misdemeanor for not reporting child abuse. He was found guilty and sentenced to two years of probation in September 2012. The court-ordered conditions required him to establish clear procedures for reporting abuse, something that many argue should have been in place all along.

Although the sentence was relatively light, the repercussions were significant. Bishop Finn stepped down from his diocesan leadership in 2015, under considerable pressure. The Vatican accepted his resignation, citing a church law that allows bishops to resign early for illness or some "grave" reason that makes them unfit for office. No specification was made about whether his legal troubles were the "grave" reason.

The case of Bishop Finn set a precedent for episcopal accountability, indicating that bishops too could face criminal charges for failing to act in cases of abuse within their jurisdictions. Though it was a watershed moment, critics argue that much more needs to be done to ensure that the Church's hierarchy is fully held to account. The case serves as a lesson in the inherent dangers of inaction, drawing attention to the urgent need for systemic change within one of the world's oldest religious institutions.

The Case of Bishop Juan Barros - A National Outcry in Chile

Bishop Juan Barros found himself at the center of Chile's sexual abuse scandal, a crisis that led to an unprecedented national questioning of the Catholic Church's authority and governance. Appointed as bishop of Osorno in 2015, Barros was immediately confronted with allegations of having covered up sexual abuse committed by Father Fernando Karadima, a highly influential priest in Chile. Victims and advocates claimed that Barros had been a witness to Karadima's abuses and had done nothing to stop him.

Despite the allegations, Barros vehemently denied any wrongdoing, leading to a situation that bitterly divided the local Catholic community. However, what made this case extraordinary was the involvement of Pope Francis, who initially defended Barros, suggesting that the accusations were "calumny." This led to a significant outcry in Chile and among victims of clergy abuse globally.

The crisis reached such proportions that Pope Francis later admitted to making "serious mistakes" in handling the case. In an about-face, he summoned all of Chile's bishops to Rome in May 2018, following which every bishop offered to resign—a move unparalleled in the modern history of the Catholic Church. Pope Francis accepted Barros's resignation in June 2018, signaling a watershed moment in the Church's attempt to be transparent about its handling of sexual abuse cases.

Cardinal Keith O'Brien - A Fall from Grace in Scotland

Cardinal Keith O'Brien was one of the most powerful figures in the Catholic Church in the UK until allegations of inappropriate sexual behavior forced his sudden resignation as Archbishop of St. Andrews and Edinburgh in 2013. Accused by several priests and a former priest of unwanted advances and inappropriate contact dating back to the 1980s, O'Brien initially contested these allegations.

However, the scenario changed dramatically when O'Brien admitted to his sexual misconduct, marking a grim chapter in the Church's history in Scotland. The Vatican acted swiftly; though O'Brien formally resigned due to age reasons, it was clear that his resignation was accelerated by the allegations. He recused himself from participating in the conclave that elected Pope Francis and withdrew from public life. Later, he renounced the rights and privileges of a cardinal, though he retained the title until his death in 2018.

Both cases underline the significant shifts occurring within the Catholic Church concerning the handling of sexual abuse allegations. No longer can high-ranking Church officials expect to be insulated from accusations and scrutiny, reflecting a broader change in attitudes both inside and outside the institution.

Archbishop Jozef Wesolowski – A Diplomatic Quandary

Archbishop Jozef Wesolowski, originally from Poland, was an influential Vatican diplomat stationed in the Dominican Republic when allegations of sexual abuse against minors emerged. As a papal nuncio—a Vatican ambassador of sorts—Wesolowski enjoyed a certain level of diplomatic immunity, which complicated efforts to hold him accountable. His case brought forth the sticky intersection of church law, international diplomacy, and criminal justice.

In 2013, he was recalled to Vatican City, ostensibly to face charges under the Church's own legal system. In a rare move, Wesolowski was laicized (defrocked) in 2014, meaning he was stripped of his clerical status. Before facing a criminal trial at the Vatican, he was arrested in Vatican City in September 2014. However, he died in 2015 before a secular court could take up his case, leaving many to wonder whether justice had indeed been served.

The Case of Cardinal Philippe Barbarin – A Landmark Verdict in France

Cardinal Philippe Barbarin, the Archbishop of Lyon, France, became a central figure in a case that tested how the Church dealt with bishops accused of covering up for abusive priests. In 2019, Barbarin was convicted for failing to report sexual abuse allegations against a priest, Bernard Preynat, who had been accused of abusing dozens of boy scouts in the 1980s and 1990s.

Barbarin's conviction was a milestone; it was one of the first times a high-ranking church official was held legally accountable for covering up abuse. Although his conviction was later overturned in appeal in 2020, Barbarin had already offered his resignation to Pope Francis, which was eventually accepted.

Cardinal Roger Mahony - A Saga of Secrecy in Los Angeles

Cardinal Roger Mahony, the long-serving Archbishop of Los Angeles, found his legacy tarnished by his role in handling multiple sexual abuse cases within his archdiocese. Documents released in 2013 indicated that Mahony and other church officials tried to shield priests accused of sexual abuse from law enforcement scrutiny in the 1980s and 1990s. The Cardinal was publicly censured by his successor, Archbishop José Gomez, and stripped of his public duties—although he remains a cardinal in good standing.

Mahony's case showed that even figures who were once nearly untouchable in the American Catholic hierarchy could face repercussions for their role in the abuse scandal. However, the repercussions have mostly been ecclesiastical rather than legal, prompting continued debates over accountability within the Church.

These cases further emphasize the labyrinthine paths that justice must navigate in the domain of the Church's internal politics and external legal systems. The dire need for a universally applicable standard of justice and transparency becomes more evident with each revelation.

The Case of Father Brendan Smyth - A Cross-Border Scandal

Father Brendan Smyth was an Irish Catholic priest whose actions precipitated one of the most significant scandals in the Catholic Church's history in Ireland, affecting both Northern Ireland and the Republic. He was a member of the Norbertine Order and served in various parishes across Ireland and the United States. Over the years, he sexually abused and assaulted perhaps hundreds of children.

The egregious nature of Smyth's actions was overshadowed only by the extensive cover-up that involved church and state institutions. His case spanned decades and involved multiple jurisdictions, making it a textbook example of how systemic failings can exacerbate individual crimes. Warnings about Smyth's behavior were effectively ignored or inadequately addressed, allowing him to continue his abuses.

Finally, in 1994, Smyth was convicted of 17 counts of child sexual abuse in Northern Ireland. He was sentenced to four years in prison. In 1997, he pleaded guilty to additional charges in the Republic of Ireland and was sentenced to 12 years in prison. Father Brendan Smyth died in prison just one month into his sentence, but the shadow of his actions continues to loom large.

His case ignited a political crisis in Ireland, leading to the collapse of the Irish government in 1994 due to its mishandling of the extradition process. This was not just a failure of a single individual but an indictment of a system that facilitated the abuse, thus shaking the public's faith in both religious and state institutions. It served as a catalyst for sweeping reforms and investigations into the Catholic Church's handling of sexual abuse allegations, not just in Ireland but worldwide.

The Case of Archbishop Anthony Apuron - A Scandal in Paradise

In the idyllic island of Guam, a U.S. territory in the western Pacific, a scandal emerged that rattled the local community and had ramifications extending all the way to the Vatican. Archbishop Anthony Apuron, the highest-ranking Catholic clergyman on the island, was accused of sexually abusing minors.

The case against Apuron was anything but straightforward. He served as Archbishop of Agaña from 1986 until 2016, when Pope Francis suspended him following the allegations. The accusations came from multiple individuals, including former altar boys who reported abuse dating back to the 1970s.

In a turn of events that showcased the Vatican's increased commitment to tackling abuse within the Church, a canonical (church law) trial was held. In 2018, a Vatican tribunal found Apuron guilty of some of the accusations against him, a decision upheld on appeal in 2019. Remarkably, this was one of the few instances where a high-ranking church official was formally tried and found guilty by the Vatican itself, and it was met with both relief and skepticism by those demanding accountability.

The tribunal stripped Apuron of his office, though he retained the title of archbishop. He was also prohibited from residing in Guam. The judgment was a watershed moment in the Church's history, as it indicated a significant—though arguably insufficient—shift toward accountability.

However, the case raised serious questions. Why did it take so long for the allegations to surface publicly? Why were the victims' voices initially met with institutional silence? The Apuron case illuminated the broader issues of power, abuse, and the severe lack of oversight within Church structures, even in such remote parts of the world. The verdict was not just an indictment against a single individual but a critique of a global institution's failures.

The Mount Cashel Orphanage Scandal: Canada's Hidden Shame

In the heart of St. John's, Newfoundland, the Mount Cashel Orphanage, run by the Christian Brothers, was long seen as a sanctuary for orphaned and neglected boys. The orphanage, active from 1875 until its closure in 1990, had enjoyed a good reputation—until it didn't.

The tale that unraveled was a harrowing narrative that destroyed the lives of countless boys and shook the Catholic Church in Canada to its core. By the late 1980s, investigations and journalistic endeavors began to reveal that the Christian Brothers, who ran the facility, had for decades subjected residents to physical, emotional, and sexual abuse.

In a devastating episode of collective trauma, victims came forward to recount abuses ranging from beatings to sexual assault. What made the Mount Cashel Orphanage case deeply disturbing was not just the scale and duration of the abuse, but also the ensuing cover-ups. Documents came to light showing that both Church and state officials were aware of the abuse allegations as early as the 1970s but failed to act upon them, let alone bring justice to the abused. In some instances, accused Brothers were merely transferred to other institutions, a disturbing pattern of "reassign and forget" that was common in many abuse cases worldwide.

The Christian Brothers declared bankruptcy, and the orphanage was eventually demolished, as if erasing its physical presence could wipe away the memories of those who suffered there. Some of the Brothers were criminally convicted, but for many, the justice was too little, too late. The harm done was irreversible, and the scandal led to a loss of faith not just in a religious institution but also in the societal structures supposed to protect the most vulnerable.

As the Royal Commission on the Mount Cashel Orphanage was set up to examine the complexities and systemic failures surrounding the scandal, Canadians had to grapple with an uncomfortable reality: that monsters could lurk behind the most sacrosanct institutions. And as much as the commission's findings offered some solace, they also laid bare the hard truth—that the scandal was less an aberration and more a horrifying symptom of a much larger, systemic problem of abuse and neglect.

The Mount Cashel tragedy remains a black mark on Canada's conscience, a grim testament to the destructive power of silence and the urgent necessity for accountability in institutions we blindly trust.

The Neerkol Orphanage Case: Australia's Dark Legacy

Nestled in the regional landscape of Rockhampton, Queensland, the St. Joseph's Orphanage at Neerkol appeared to be an idyllic setting for children who had lost their families or were unable to live with them. However, beneath the veneer of tranquility lay an abyss of sorrow and mistreatment.

Founded in 1885 by the Catholic Church, the Neerkol Orphanage was the epicenter of a hidden tragedy that unfolded over decades. Hundreds of children, many of them indigenous, were placed under the care of nuns and priests who were supposed to provide a nurturing environment. But instead, these young souls found themselves entrapped in a nightmare of sexual, physical, and psychological abuse.

As early as the 1940s, the first threads of the devastating tapestry began to emerge. Yet it wasn't until the late 1990s that the abuse received public attention, largely thanks to the tireless efforts of survivors and investigative journalists. Horrific accounts started to surface, ranging from severe beatings and forced labor to sexual assault. These weren't isolated incidents but rather systemic abuses that penetrated the very core of the institution.

Particularly striking was the collusion between church officials and local authorities, creating a wall of silence around the orphanage that was nearly impossible to penetrate. This layer of institutional protection allowed the atrocities to continue largely unchecked for years, and any attempt at exposure was swiftly suppressed.

When the dam finally broke, the revelations led to a series of legal proceedings and public inquiries, including the Royal Commission into Institutional Responses to Child Sexual Abuse. Yet justice remains elusive. Although some individuals were prosecuted, the systemic issues continue to persist, requiring a more significant reckoning.

The Neerkol Orphanage case serves as a grim testament to the capacity for abuse within trusted institutions, a chilling narrative of what can happen when those with power are allowed to operate without oversight or accountability. As Australia grapples with the weight of this legacy, the scandal serves as a cautionary tale, urging society to question the sanctity of institutions and to relentlessly pursue truth, however uncomfortable it may be.

Salesians of Don Bosco Scandal: A Global Crisis of Trust

The Salesians of Don Bosco, founded by Saint John Bosco in the 19th century, hold a storied reputation for their commitment to the education and betterment of young people, particularly those who are disadvantaged. With operations in over 130 countries, this Catholic religious institute has an expansive reach. However, that very reach has become a point of contention, as allegations of sexual abuse have emerged from multiple locations worldwide, tarnishing the Salesian name and undermining the mission they claim to uphold.

The scope of the scandal is as wide as the organization itself, stretching from Europe to the Americas, from Africa to Asia. Members of the Salesian order have been implicated in a series of abuse cases, some of which span decades. The accusations range from inappropriate sexual conduct and grooming to full-blown sexual assault of minors, often taking place under the guise of spiritual guidance or educational mentorship.

While the individual cases are egregious, the collective pattern they reveal is even more alarming. Far from being isolated incidents, the abuses seem to point to systemic issues within the Salesian organization, such as the failure to report allegations to appropriate authorities and a culture of secrecy that protects perpetrators at the expense of victims. When some cases did manage to surface, the organization's frequent response was to transfer the accused to a different location—a maneuver that not only evaded legal consequences but also exposed a new community to potential abuse.

Attempts to reckon with the scandal have been complicated by the Salesians' global presence, which enables jurisdictional ambiguities. National and international authorities have been slow to intervene, partly because religious organizations often operate in a quasi-autonomous capacity, a condition that complicates legal enforcement.

That said, some progress has been made. In the United States and Australia, for instance, court proceedings have led to convictions and financial settlements for victims. Public inquiries, like the Royal Commission into Institutional Responses to Child Sexual Abuse in Australia, have also included investigations into Salesian-run institutions.

However, for the Salesian scandal to truly be addressed, what's required is nothing short of a profound organizational reckoning—a radical introspection that grapples with the paradox of an entity committed to youth welfare while simultaneously endangering it. Until then, the Salesians of Don Bosco remain a case study in how an organization's lofty aims can be undermined by a deeply rooted culture of abuse and secrecy.

The Case of Father Oliver O'Grady: A Documentary Indictment

Father Oliver O'Grady, an Irish-born priest who served in multiple parishes across California, became the sinister face of clerical sexual abuse for many after his life and crimes were exposed in the 2006 documentary "Deliver Us from Evil." This film not only elucidated the scale of O'Grady's abuse but also magnified the systemic failings of the Catholic Church in dealing with such predators within their ranks.

O'Grady's actions were nothing short of horrific, encompassing a wide array of abuses against children, including both boys and girls, some as young as nine months old. But what made this case especially chilling was O'Grady's seeming nonchalance about his crimes. The documentary features interviews where he calmly describes his actions, expressing minimal remorse. His demeanor suggests a man detached from the gravity of his sins, a trait that can't help but provoke revulsion and disbelief.

However, the scope of the tragedy extends beyond just O'Grady. The Church hierarchy, particularly within the Diocese of Stockton where he served, exhibited a remarkable capacity for moral evasion. Despite multiple allegations and settlements, O'Grady was simply moved from parish to parish, a practice known as "clerical shifting," thereby enabling his continued abuse. In this way, the Church's administrative structure acted as a protective shell around him.

Legal consequences for O'Grady came in the form of various lawsuits and a criminal conviction in 1993 for molestation, leading to his imprisonment for seven years. After serving his sentence, he was deported to Ireland. However, the notion of justice in this context feels pyrrhic, as no amount of legal reprisal could ever truly compensate for the trauma inflicted on his victims.

Beyond the personal tales of suffering, O'Grady's story, accentuated by its cinematic depiction, pushed the conversation about clerical abuse into the global spotlight. It confronted audiences with the uncomfortable truth that perpetrators are not always shadowy figures lurking on the periphery, but can also be individuals who stand at the very pulpits that are supposed to symbolize moral certitude.

The case of Father Oliver O'Grady acts as a harrowing reminder of the twofold failure in dealing with clerical abuse: individual malfeasance, undoubtedly, but also a collective institutional betrayal that amplifies the tragedy manifold.

St. John's School for the Deaf, Milwaukee: A Silent Nightmare

One of the most harrowing cases of clerical abuse unfolded in an unlikely sanctuary of education and faith: St. John's School for the Deaf in Milwaukee. At the center of this storm was Father Lawrence Murphy, a man who used his position to exploit the most vulnerable of victims—children who were deaf.

From the 1950s through the 1970s, Father Lawrence Murphy was a dominant figure at St. John's, where he served as the director. He had a deep influence not just on the institution but also on the students who saw him as a spiritual guide, a teacher, and, tragically, as someone who should have been a protector. Father Murphy abused at least 200 deaf boys during his tenure, according to the accounts that emerged years later.

What made this case uniquely cruel was the abuse of trust perpetrated in a setting where communication was already a challenge. Many of the children couldn't effectively convey what had happened to them due to limitations in their ability to speak or write. The very conditions that made St. John's a necessary sanctuary for these children also made it a predator's playground.

Murphy, like other clerical offenders, seemed to act with a sense of impunity, enabled, in part, by the institutional structures around him. Reports suggest that several archbishops and even the Vatican had been notified of his actions as early as the 1950s. While Murphy was removed from his post in 1974, he was never defrocked or arrested. Instead, he was moved to another diocese where he continued to work with children and, purportedly, continued his predatory behavior.

The psychological toll of Murphy's actions reverberated through the lives of his victims in ways that are almost unimaginable. The trauma was exacerbated by the Church's long failure to act decisively, which gave victims the impression that their suffering was of little concern to an institution that was supposed to provide moral leadership.

Father Lawrence Murphy died in 1998, never having faced a criminal trial. However, his story became part of a larger societal reckoning when it was featured in the 2012 documentary "Mea Maxima Culpa: Silence in the House of God." The film did more than just narrate the individual stories of abuse; it underscored the dire need for systemic change within religious organizations.

The case of St. John's School for the Deaf serves as a sobering testament to the horrific depths that can be reached when those in positions of power are allowed to exploit the vulnerable. It also underscores the essential need for institutions to not just preach moral principles, but to act on them—especially when the lives and well-being of innocent children are at stake.

The Altoona-Johnstown Diocese Scandal: A Catastrophic Betrayal of Trust

Pennsylvania's Altoona-Johnstown Diocese scandal, unearthed through a grand jury report, unveiled one of the most extensive and deeply entrenched networks of abuse within the Catholic Church in the United States. The findings, published in 2016, documented horrific instances of sexual abuse by at least 50 priests and religious leaders over a span of several decades.

The victims, numbering in the hundreds, were predominantly children and teenagers who had turned to the Church for solace and spiritual guidance. Instead, they were subjected to sexual exploitation and manipulation that left lasting scars on their lives. The grand jury report was a testament to their courage in coming forward to share their stories, many of which had been suppressed by fear, shame, and the relentless tactics of their abusers.

What made this scandal especially alarming was the extent to which church officials, including bishops, actively engaged in covering up the abuse. Reports detailed how known offenders were shuffled between parishes or sent for treatment with no legal consequences, effectively allowing them to continue their predation on new victims. This pattern of evasion and complicity reached the highest echelons of the diocese, where protecting the reputation of the Church took precedence over the protection of innocent lives.

The grand jury report also exposed the alarming inadequacies of both state and church authorities in addressing the crisis. Statutes of limitations and legal loopholes had shielded many perpetrators from prosecution, and the secrecy of church proceedings had prevented the truth from coming to light for decades.

As the report was made public, it sent shockwaves throughout Pennsylvania and beyond. It triggered a renewed urgency for justice and accountability, prompting legal reforms and legislative changes aimed at eliminating legal barriers to prosecuting perpetrators. It also fueled the broader conversation about the need for transparency and oversight within religious institutions, challenging the deference and privilege that had historically shielded them from scrutiny.

The Case of Father Normand J. Roger: A Predator in Priest's Clothing

In the tranquil state of Maine, beneath the façade of religious devotion and spiritual leadership, a disturbing tale of abuse unfolded—one that centered around Father Normand J. Roger, a Catholic priest who violated the sacred trust of his position.

Father Roger, ordained in 1968, served in various parishes within the Roman Catholic Diocese of Portland, Maine. To the unsuspecting faithful, he was a figure of authority, guiding their spiritual journeys and officiating over important life events. However, beneath the priestly vestments, Roger harbored a dark secret: a penchant for sexually abusing children.

The details of Roger's crimes are chilling. Over the course of his priesthood, he targeted young boys, often gaining access to them through his position within the Church. He used his authority and influence to groom his victims, exploiting their trust and vulnerability. The abuse was not an isolated incident but a pattern of predation that spanned years.

It was only in the early 1990s that Roger's heinous acts began to come to light. Survivors began to break their silence, bravely sharing their stories and seeking justice. Legal authorities took action, and in 1993, Roger was arrested and subsequently convicted on charges related to child sexual abuse. He was sentenced to prison, a rare occurrence in cases involving abusive clergy members.

The conviction of Father Normand J. Roger was a testament to the resilience and courage of his survivors, who had the strength to confront their abuser and demand justice. It also underscored the importance of accountability within religious institutions. The case sent a powerful message that no one, regardless of their position, should be immune from the consequences of their actions.

However, it's essential to recognize that while Roger faced legal repercussions, the scars inflicted on his victims and the broader community endure. The case serves as a stark reminder of the profound harm that can be wrought by individuals who exploit their positions of trust and authority, and it highlights the critical need for vigilance and safeguards to protect the vulnerable from those who would prey upon them.

The Case of Father Rudy Kos: From the Pulpit to a Life Sentence

In the heart of Dallas, Texas, the case of Father Rudy Kos unfolded as a devastating reminder that evil can lurk even within the sanctuaries of faith. Father Kos, a Catholic priest ordained in 1972, served in various parishes within the Dallas Diocese. To the congregation, he was a trusted spiritual leader, offering guidance and solace in times of need. Yet, beneath his clerical robes, he harbored a dark secret—a predilection for sexual abuse that spanned decades.

Kos's crimes were horrifying. He preyed upon young boys, exploiting their trust and vulnerability, often using his position of authority within the Church to gain access to his victims. His pattern of abuse was not limited to one parish or one period but extended over many years, leaving a trail of pain and suffering in its wake.

The first allegations against Kos began to surface in the early 1990s, when survivors summoned the courage to break their silence. They came forward, sharing their harrowing stories and seeking justice. Legal authorities took action, and in 1998, Father Rudy Kos faced criminal charges related to child sexual abuse.

In a landmark trial, Kos was convicted and sentenced to life imprisonment in 1999. This outcome was a testament to the resilience and bravery of his survivors, who demonstrated extraordinary strength in confronting their abuser and demanding justice.

The case of Father Rudy Kos serves as a stark reminder that the abuse of power and the violation of trust can occur even within the holiest of institutions. It underscores the importance of accountability and transparency within religious organizations, as well as the critical need to protect the most vulnerable members of the community from those who would exploit their faith and innocence.

While Kos faced legal consequences for his actions, it's essential to acknowledge that the scars inflicted upon his victims endure. Their courage in coming forward not only brought their abuser to justice but also shed light on the broader issue of clergy abuse, prompting discussions and reforms within the Catholic Church and society at large.

The Case of Father James Porter: A Predator's Reign of Terror

In the annals of clergy abuse, few cases are as shocking and disturbing as that of Father James Porter, a Catholic priest whose reign of terror left a trail of devastation and shattered lives across Massachusetts.

Ordained as a priest in 1960, Porter's clerical career began seemingly innocently, as he served in various parishes within the Fall River Diocese.

However, beneath his priestly vestments lurked a monster—a man who preyed upon the most vulnerable members of his flock, particularly children.

Porter's crimes were nothing short of horrifying. He was accused of sexually abusing more than 100 children during his time as a priest. His victims were both boys and girls, and the abuse took various forms, including molestation and rape. What made his actions even more appalling was the deliberate and calculated manner in which he groomed and manipulated his young victims.

The first allegations against Porter emerged in the early 1960s, but his superiors in the Catholic Church failed to take decisive action. Instead of removing him from ministry and reporting his crimes to the authorities, he was simply transferred to different parishes—a practice known as "clerical shifting." This allowed him to continue his reign of terror unabated, and he continued to exploit his position of trust to gain access to new victims.

It wasn't until the mid-1990s that the full extent of Porter's crimes began to come to light. Survivors, who had lived for decades with the trauma inflicted by their abuser, began to break their silence. Their courage in sharing their stories finally led to legal action against Porter.

In 1993, Porter was convicted on multiple counts of sexual abuse and sentenced to prison. His conviction sent shockwaves through the Catholic Church and society at large, prompting a renewed urgency to confront the issue of clergy abuse and to seek justice for survivors.

The case of Father James Porter is a stark reminder of the grave consequences that can result from the failure of institutions to protect the vulnerable and to hold abusers accountable. It also highlights the profound bravery of survivors who, despite the passage of time, found the strength to speak out and demand justice.

The Case of Father Alfred J. Bietighofer: A Congregation's Betrayal

Father Alfred J. Bietighofer, a Catholic priest in Connecticut, held a position of trust and reverence within his congregation. Ordained in 1966, he was expected to embody the highest moral and ethical standards. However, beneath his clerical collar lay a deeply troubling secret—a pattern of alleged sexual abuse that would eventually expose a betrayal of trust.

Accusations against Father Bietighofer began to emerge in the late 1980s, when several survivors summoned the courage to come forward. These individuals, who had been parishioners and students under his care, claimed that they had been sexually abused by the priest during their formative years. The allegations were shocking, involving both boys and girls.

What was particularly disturbing about the case was the apparent disregard for the welfare of victims within the Catholic Church's hierarchy. Despite multiple allegations against Bietighofer, he was allowed to continue his ministry, moving from one parish to another. This practice of transferring abusive priests to different locations, a strategy known as "clerical shifting," enabled him to continue his alleged predation unchecked.

The survivors' stories eventually gained traction in the early 2000s, leading to legal action against Father Bietighofer. In 2003, he was arrested and charged with multiple counts of sexual abuse. The case represented a reckoning for both the priest and the Church, which had failed to protect its most vulnerable members.

In 2005, Father Bietighofer was convicted of sexual assault and risk of injury to a minor. He was sentenced to prison, marking a significant step toward justice for his survivors. The conviction also served as a reminder that no one, regardless of their position, should be above the law.

37

A Veil of Silence

In the dimly lit halls of ecclesiastical bureaucracy, a phenomenon thrives like fungi in the shadows—clericalism. This term refers to an undue deference toward clergy, a cultural acceptance of a priest's word as infallible and an assumption that they are above reproach. With clericalism as a backdrop, the Church has also employed what it calls "pontifical secrecy," a practice intended to protect sensitive church matters but one that has been conveniently wielded to shield allegations of abuse.

Clericalism: The Unholy Shield

Clericalism serves as an ideological shield that protects perpetrators from scrutiny. Those within the Church who question the conduct of their superiors are often met with repercussions that range from subtle ostracization to blatant career sabotage. For the laity, clericalism instills a debilitating sense of powerlessness. How can you question a man who is perceived as a conduit to the divine?

Pontifical Secrecy: Silence by Decree

Under the veil of pontifical secrecy, bishops and cardinals are bound to a solemn code that inhibits them from disclosing sensitive information—even if it involves allegations of abuse. Up until recently, this ecclesiastical rule has functioned as a legal gag order, fostering an environment where the perpetrator's reputation is deemed more important than delivering justice to victims.

115

38

Shifting the Blame

"The lady doth protest too much, methinks," muses Queen Gertrude in Shakespeare's *Hamlet*, suspecting that overemphasized innocence betrays guilt. Such a sentiment can be applied to how some factions within the Church have reacted to the crisis. Instead of introspection, these quarters have often engaged in victim-blending or blaming societal decay for their internal failings.

Victim-Blaming: A Sinful Diversion

Some Church representatives have gone so far as to cast aspersions on the victims themselves. Accusations against the abused range from them "tempting" the priests to being unreliable witnesses due to trauma or emotional instability. This strategy doesn't just add insult to injury; it perpetuates a cycle where victims are silenced and potential future victims are put at risk.

The "Moral Decline" Fallacy

When the lens of blame turns outward, some Church spokespeople attribute the crisis to an external "moral decline" in society. By positing that priests are not the perpetrators but the victims of a godless culture, this argument absolves the institution of its need to reform. It's akin to blaming the sea for the shipwreck, conveniently ignoring the gaping holes in the ship's hull.

39

Lack of Accountability

The issue of sexual abuse within the Church isn't just shrouded in moral ambiguity but also in a fog of data obscurity. The absence of comprehensive, transparent data collection is both a symptom of the institution's systemic failures and a roadblock to lasting solutions.

The Black Hole of Data

Within the fortified walls of Vatican City, there's a peculiar irony: an institution that has meticulously recorded centuries of liturgical texts, theological arguments, and historical events appears significantly less committed to keeping accurate data on abuse cases. This lapse serves a dual purpose. First, the absence of data prevents the full scale of the problem from coming into light, effectively minimizing the urgency to act. Second, without data, any discussion about the prevalence and patterns of abuse remains anecdotal, making systemic change difficult to strategize.

The Vatican's Resistance to Transparency

In an era where transparency is increasingly valued, and sometimes even demanded by the public, the Vatican's hesitance to be fully transparent about the scope of abuse is unsettling. This resistance has often led to what can be described as "patchwork solutions"—measures that address individual cases without confronting the root issues. The problem with patchwork solutions is that while they may offer temporary relief or give the appearance of action, they do little to prevent future abuses or repair the institutional failures that allowed the abuses to happen in the first place.

Incomplete Measures: The Illusion of Action

A review board here, an internal investigation there—these are steps, yes, but they often function as mere window dressing. Most of these measures lack any independent oversight or checks and balances. As a result, the Church remains the investigator, judge, and jury in cases of alleged abuse within its walls—a clear conflict of interest that undermines any push toward real accountability.

The Conundrum of Canon Law

The Church's own legal system, Canon Law, often serves as another obstacle to accountability. Designed to address spiritual matters, Canon Law is ill-equipped to handle the intricacies and ethical obligations involved in criminal cases of abuse. Relying solely on Canon Law for internal investigations and disciplinary actions effectively places these severe offenses in a legal limbo, beyond the reach of secular justice systems.

In sum, the lack of accountability doesn't merely stem from individual failings but is a consequence of institutional choices—choices that prioritize the Church's reputation over the well-being of its most vulnerable members.

40

Toward Redemption? Attempts at Resolution and Reparation

The complexity of the sexual abuse crisis within the Catholic Church defies simple solutions. Nevertheless, various attempts at resolution and reparation have been made, some more effective than others. In this section, we'll examine the contours of these efforts and evaluate whether they're mere drops in an ocean of systemic failures or meaningful strides toward institutional redemption.

Papal Acknowledgment

The Papacy has long served as the moral and spiritual compass for millions of Catholics worldwide. So, when the Pope speaks, people listen. Popes John Paul II, Benedict XVI, and Francis have all acknowledged the sexual abuse crisis, albeit with varying degrees of urgency and introspection. While Pope John Paul II's stance was often criticized for its minimalism, Pope Francis has been more proactive in addressing the issue, calling for "an all-out battle against the abuse of minors."

But what impact do these Papal acknowledgments really have? They certainly make headlines and offer some level of validation to victims, but do they inspire effective action? The varied responses from dioceses and religious orders worldwide suggest that a Papal nod, while necessary, is far from sufficient.

The Legal Landscape

Parallel to the Church's internal reviews and Papal pronouncements, the secular legal systems of various countries have increasingly played a role. Lawsuits in the United States, criminal investigations in Australia, and inquiries in Ireland and the UK reveal a global desire for justice that transcends religious boundaries. These efforts are not just about bringing perpetrators to justice but also about holding the institution accountable for enabling and concealing abuse.

However, the Vatican's relationship with these legal proceedings has been complex. Despite calling for accountability, the Holy See has often employed diplomatic channels to protect its clergy from prosecution, citing sovereign immunity. This tension between legal responsibility and institutional protection remains a significant hurdle on the road to true accountability and reform.

Restorative Justice

While legal measures aim to penalize and deter, restorative justice seeks to heal. Financial reparations, although incapable of undoing the emotional and psychological trauma, offer a form of tangible acknowledgment. Programs for therapy and counseling for victims mark another crucial step.

However, restorative justice must extend beyond these individual measures to address the systemic nature of the problem. This would involve not just financial reparations but also a significant overhaul of internal Church policies on reporting abuse, vetting seminarians, and providing pastoral care for communities affected by abuse.